A NEW ADDITION TO THE SUCC

SAT ATTAC__

BADGER KS3 TEST GUIDES

ASSESS
MUCH ADO
ABOUT NOTHING
WITH FOCUS 2007

JONATHAN MORGAN

Supplies of ammunition included to help make the Shakespeare paper *Mission Possible* for your students!

**Badger
Publishing**

Assess
MUCH ADO ABOUT NOTHING
with Focus
2007

Contents

Chapter	Section	Page reference
1	Introduction – how to use this resource book effectively	3-7
2	Commentary on the whole play	8-15
3	Key scenes with explanation and glossary	16-29
4	Exploring the key scenes 50 probing questions	30-38
5	Explaining the assessment focuses	39-48
6	Responding to the assessment focuses	49-63
7	Exam preparation	64-71
8	Sample exam questions	72-82
9	Marks scheme, including explanation and exemplar responses	83-87

Chapter 1

Introduction

This resource book has been designed to provide your students with all the support required for their *MUCH ADO ABOUT NOTHING* reading paper for 2007.

Outline of the 2007 exam

The way that the papers are assessed is shown below. Notice how much percentage is given to each section; this should determine how much time should be allocated. The Shakespeare paper is only worth 18% of the overall mark. However, it is still an area which requires the most explanation because of the language barrier that many students have difficulty with.

		Marks awarded (%)	Time given
Two Reading Papers	Reading Booklet	32	1 hour 15 minutes
	Shakespeare	18	45 minutes
One Writing Paper	Longer Writing	30	45 minutes
	Shorter Writing	20	30 minutes

MUCH ADO 2007
© BADGER PUBLISHING

Assess Much Ado about Nothing with Focus has the following aims:

- Provide detailed commentaries on every aspect of the key scenes, including explanations of important words and phrases.

- Develop students' understanding of the key scenes through a series of probing questions – related to the main themes and ideas in the scenes as well exploring characterisation and dramatic devices.

- Inform teachers and students of the assessment focuses, as well as providing exemplar responses and student directed questions for the set scenes.

- Prepare students for the directing the scenes question. All the key areas of staging will be considered, which should allow students to feel well-equipped in their Shakespeare exam.

- Encourage students to structure their ideas clearly in an exam. There are sample essay plans and exemplar responses as well as writing frames and examiner tips on how to communicate clearly.

- Provide examples of the type of question that will be asked in the 2007 exam. Five sample exam questions have been written in the same style and layout as the real exam.

- Explain how students are assessed. There is a detailed mark scheme for reading as well as examples of students' work at each level.

How should I use this resource book effectively?

Supporting teachers

This resource book is not designed to tell your students everything they need to know about Shakespeare or, indeed, *MUCH ADO ABOUT NOTHING*. As the title suggests, it is focused directly on the key scenes and the way that your students are assessed in their Shakespeare exam. Introductions to Shakespeare are mostly done in primary school or in Years 7 and 8; therefore, avoid wasting time on basic introductions to Shakespeare such as time lines, a guide to the Elizabethan theatre, etc - these should be evident in earlier schemes of work. When planning, provide some opportunities for students to recount their knowledge in the form of a KWL grid:

- What do students already know?
- What do they want to find out?
- What have they learnt?

One of the important decisions teachers need to make is how they cover the play in a short time-frame, especially as it is only worth 18 marks and 18% of the final grade awarded; spending only 18% of your time on Shakespeare may seem numerically wise, yet consideration must also be given to the language barrier that students face when approaching the exam, as well as navigating through various scenes in a short time. It is advisable to avoid reading the whole play, although students will need to know how the key scenes impact on the plot and character development as well as how they link to the major themes of the play; use the summary sheets before reading the key scenes in order to familiarise students with the main events and how the key scenes fit into the bigger picture.

If there are teachers in the department who are unfamiliar with the Shakespeare exam then it is vital that you share the book with them during a department meeting. They will need to understand how to approach *MUCH ADO ABOUT NOTHING* with the key scenes and exam requirements in mind; in particular, the importance of approaching the assessment focuses needs to be addressed so that both teachers and students feel well-equipped to tackle the paper. It is advisable that there is a common approach to preparing the students for the exam itself as it will allow for standardisation and moderation of students' work.

Supporting learning in the classroom

Initially, it is important to re-introduce Shakespeare to the students - perhaps using more inventive ways than Research Shakespeare - reams of Encarta sheets later and you will understand why there should be more focus. Try to use the existing knowledge in the classroom - you may be surprised how much students may already know about *MUCH ADO ABOUT NOTHING*.

MUCH ADO 2007

© BADGER PUBLISHING

With regards to the themes of the play, it is advisable to show how *MUCH ADO ABOUT NOTHING* has cultural relevance; isolate the broad themes and put them in a modern context so that students can begin to engage in the dilemmas and conflicts that the characters face. Consider the important issues of love and marriage, gender battles, family conflicts, deception, class differences, etc, then relate these to the students' own experience - this should help them identify with Shakespeare's purpose and cultural relevance.

One technique that could be used to engage students with the language of the play is to use the glossary sections from the key scenes in a card-sort/matching game. It is best to use this technique before you read the scenes (don't tell them they are from the scenes) in a fairly light-hearted manner – perhaps a series of starters or oral plenaries. In this way, students will hopefully be aware of the complex language before reading the scenes, albeit subconsciously. When doing the card-sort activity, explore the language with the students through spelling strategies so they will feel more confident in establishing the meaning of Shakespeare's language; it is hoped that this approach may help students to feel less intimidated by the language and perhaps lift that particular barrier to learning.

Once students are familiar with the plot of *MUCH ADO ABOUT NOTHING*, have explored the themes and begun to tackle the language of the key scenes, it is time to begin reading and exploring the scenes themselves. There are various ways to do this:

1. Read the scenes as a whole (without interruption or explanation), allowing students to engage in the mood and atmosphere of the play without disrupting the flow.

2. Break the scenes into shorter manageable sections (as shown in Chapter 6).

The choice will depend on the nature of students and their understanding of the language - if teachers feel that interruptions will ruin the flow and cause confusion, then choose option 1. If it is clear that students have switched off because of the need for explanation, choose option 2.

Exploring the key scenes

In Chapter 4, *Exploring the key scenes*, there are a number of questions set for each key scene, none of which are solely testing comprehension. These tasks will require a great deal of thought, analysis and examination of the text. It is advisable to use the example given before each set of questions on how students should answer a question correctly.

The assessment focuses

- Motivation and behaviour
- Ideas, themes and issues
- The language of the text
- The text in performance

Inform students that the question in their exam will be based on one of these areas; therefore they need to analyse and revise the key scenes with this in mind. Teachers should use the advice and exemplars in Chapter 5 to model how students can make notes on the key scenes using the assessment focuses. Avoid giving out completed notes as students may interpret this as their revision being done for them – only use the note-making examples as a guide for shared, modelled and guided work. Effective teaching and learning should include elements of guided, shared and modelled work; therefore teachers should use Chapter 6 to support this.

Exam preparation

In Chapter 7 there is detailed advice on how to approach an exam question, plan an answer and write an effective essay, using an essay plan. These sections are crucial elements of *Assess MUCH ADO ABOUT NOTHING with Focus* and should not be left to just before the exam. Students should be given advice regularly on how to navigate their way around the exam (use last year's paper and test-base). In Chapters 8 and 9 there are five sample exam questions, including a mark scheme (explained) and exemplar responses.

Many students underachieve in this exam because they are unable to:

1) access the question;

2) plan effectively;

3) stay focused on the question set.

It is vital that students are given numerous assessment opportunities in order to establish what issues they may have with the exam procedure. Students do not need to complete sample exam after sample exam – teachers may simply ask them to make notes on the exam questions and produce sample essay plans (give time restrictions in order to recreate an exam situation).

Supporting Assessment for Learning

The large majority of schools have opted for AFL as their whole school focus; therefore it is advisable to make clear how you are supporting the whole school initiative within English planning. This book has many examples of how assessment criteria can be used for learning rather than simply a diagnostic tool. Sharing the learning objectives with students is crucial, as is demonstrating how to unpick the mark scheme and apply it through peer and self-assessment. When planning, consider how students performed in last year's paper (use PAT analysis to help with this as well as sampling from last year's papers). Adapt planning for Year 9 based on this and include curricular targets for Year 9 based on these findings.

Overall, it is hoped that this book will provide focused support on the set scenes so that students feel well-equipped for whatever Shakespeare question comes their way.

Chapter 2
Detailed scene by scene commentary

Act 1

Scene 1: Key Scene (Lines 1-123)

The play opens in Messina with Leonato, the governor of Messina, awaiting the arrival of Don Pedro, the Prince of Aragon, and his followers. His daughter, Hero, and niece, Beatrice, also anticipate the arrival of the princes who are arriving from a victorious battle. We hear about young Claudio, who is applauded for his bravery in battle in spite of his tender years. When Beatrice speaks, is it clear that there is a deep rivalry with Benedick – a "merry war" as Leonato describes it.

The men arrive, including Don John, the bastard brother of Don Pedro, who has been recently reconciled. There is a polite and courtly exchange between the characters, except Beatrice and Benedick who engage in a quarrel of vicious insults, communicated mostly through puns and word play. Benedick believes he is loved by all ladies, Beatrice excepted, and he shares the same aim as Beatrice in that they vow never to get married.

Claudio, clearly in love with Hero, asks Benedick's opinion of her which results in a scornful and sarcastic reply from Benedick, who is fearful the young lord doesn't wish to stay a bachelor. Don Pedro suggests that Benedick will fall in love soon yet he is determined to never fall victim of Cupid. When Benedick leaves, Don Pedro agrees to tell Hero and Leonato of Claudio's love and plans to pretend he is the prince at a masked ball

Scene 2

Leonato is mistakenly informed by Antonio (his older brother) that Don Pedro plans to woo Hero for himself. This news was the result of a servant overhearing the conversation and Leonato plans to prepare his daughter for Don Pedro's proposal. This old-fashioned and sexist arrangement is in sharp contrast to the independent and free spirited attitude demonstrated by Beatrice earlier in the play.

MUCH ADO 2007
© BADGER PUBLISHING

Scene 3

Don John, the illegitimate brother of Don Pedro, is unhappy and frustrated with the merry goings on around him. His friend Conrad warns him about crossing his brother again, especially as he has just recently been accepted back into the family; however, Don John is determined to be a villain and awaits an opportunity to exercise his deep rooted malice and jealousy. This duly arrives when Borachio brings news that Don Pedro plans to woo Hero on behalf of Claudio. Don John is particularly jealous of the young Claudio as he has been widely praised by his brother, Don Pedro.

Act 2 Summary

Scene 1: Key Scene (Lines 183-end)

Beatrice and Hero speak of the depressing and sour appearance of Don John. A cross between him and Benedick, comments Beatrice, would be ideal, as one never speaks and other speaks too much. Leonato and Antonio, her father, jokingly discuss marriage with Beatrice, who remains determined she will never marry. The contrast between Hero, who will obey her father's wishes, and Beatrice, who will ignore any attempts at control, is made clear in this scene.

The masked ball begins with the flirtatious exchanges between the pairs of dancers – this gives the characters the opportunity to reveal their true feelings without embarrassment. Beatrice and Benedick meet and pretend they do not recognise each other. What follows is a quite vicious verbal attack by Beatrice who calls him the "Prince's jester" and a "dull fool" among other insults. Seeking his opportunity, through the disguise of the mask, Don John tells Claudio that Don Pedro is wooing Hero for himself; Claudio believes this story instantly and is depressed, revealing his rather shallow and vulnerable nature. Claudio confides in Benedick who is himself upset because of the unpleasant comments Beatrice made against him. Claudio leaves, feeling betrayed and devastated.

MUCH ADO 2007
© BADGER PUBLISHING

Act 2, Scene 1 (cont.)

When Don Pedro arrives, he is surprised to hear of Claudio's melancholy disposition and Benedick's accusation that he has been wooing Hero for himself, which he denies, promising to return the "bird's nest" (Hero) to her rightful owner (Claudio). Benedick also continues to show how upset and angry he is at Beatrice's treatment of him, and decides to leave abruptly on her arrival with Claudio. The young prince is sad and jealous yet Don Pedro assures him that Hero has been "won" in his name and the marriage has been agreed. Claudio is unable to speak because of his immense happiness.

In contrast to this courtly and traditional exchange, Beatrice continues to be anti-marriage, refusing Don Pedro's rather insincere proposal; she comments also that she gave her heart to Benedick once yet he lost it, implying a previous relationship. The eager Claudio wishes to marry the next day yet Leonato wishes to wait a week for preparations to be complete; in the meantime, believing that Beatrice would make an excellent wife for Benedick, the princes plan to devise a plan to bring the couple together which has the approval and support of Hero, who would like to find a good husband for her cousin.

Scene 2

Don John and Borachio devise a plan to disgrace Hero, resulting in the failed marriage of Claudio and Hero. Borachio plans to be with Margaret outside a window, which will look as if Hero is entertaining another man; once this is complete, Don John will tell the princes that Hero is nothing better than a common prostitute.

Scene 3

Benedick, alone, laments at his friend Claudio's change since he fell in love; as a result, he is even more determined to keep himself away from women yet still decides to list all the qualities he would expect in one if they were lucky enough to have him. Leonato and Claudio approach and Benedick decides to hide away while complaining about Balthasar's song about men being deceivers.

Act 2, Scene 3 (cont.)

Leonato then begins to invent the story that Beatrice has fallen in love with Benedick (knowing he can overhear). Even though Benedick is shocked by this, he trusts the word of Leonato, who continues to comment that Beatrice is tormenting herself with love for Benedick, keeping herself awake writing love letters. They claim that they want to tell Benedick yet are fearful that he will mock her and reject her; moreover, they feel that he does not deserve a woman like Beatrice; aside, the two princes plan the same treatment and entrapment of Beatrice with the help of Hero.

On his own, Benedick reveals that he clearly believes what he has been told, and rather than reject Beatrice and maintain his previous position to stay single, he plans to return her 'love'. Marriage, it seems, is an attractive option now, even though he knows he will have to face the scorn of his friends. Beatrice has been sent on an errand to call him to dinner and is as antagonistic as ever; however, Benedick, clearly fallen for the trick, misinterprets her words as a sign of affection.

Act 3 Summary

Scene 1

Hero and Ursula now plan to trick Beatrice in the same way that Benedick was fooled into falling in love. They comment that Claudio and Don Pedro are convinced of Benedick's devotion to Beatrice yet are fearful that she will reject him and scorn him for this. They also comment on Benedick's good qualities and say they would rather Benedick die unloved than be a victim of Beatrice's likely disdain and rejection.

When alone, Beatrice cannot believe what she has heard and vows to say goodbye to contempt and return the 'affections' of Benedick.

Scene 2

Don Pedro chooses Benedick to go to Aragon with him as Claudio will soon be married. Benedick admits to not being himself and Don Pedro and Claudio play on his vulnerability, mocking him for being love-sick.

Don John arrives and accuses Hero of being with another man; Claudio and Don Pedro do not believe this at first yet are invited to witness Hero's 'crime'.

© BADGER PUBLISHING

Scene 3

Dogberry and Verges are the constables for the Watch who are charged with keeping the peace in the night; it is clear that these characters are figures of fun and provide the light entertainment of the play, commenting that the drunks should stay drunk and it's better to allow thieves to do as they wish. This provides the audience with some light relief from the serious events of the previous scene and the events that are to follow. While they are waiting, a drunken Borachio and Conrad approach, with the former boasting that he has earned money from working with Don John.

We discover that Margaret had worn Hero's clothes and was seen with Borachio by Claudio and Don Pedro, who believed that it was Hero who had been entertaining a man. The watchmen also overhear Borachio admitting that he has helped the plot to destroy the marriage; Claudio, we hear, plans to disgrace Hero at the planned marriage. The watchmen finally arrest Borachio and Conrad.

Scene 4

The planned wedding day of Hero and Claudio. Hero is getting ready for the marriage when Beatrice arrives, clearly not herself, even suggesting that she may be ready for a husband. Hero and Margaret say that the cure for her ills is a medicine called 'Benedictus', to which she responds favourably.

Scene 5

Leonato is approached by Dogberry and Verges, who plan to tell the Prince about the plot against Hero and the arrest of Borachio and Conrad. Leonato asks the watchmen to question the villains themselves as he is in a rush to get to church and it is also difficult to understand what they are actually saying.

Act 4 Summary

Scene 1

The wedding service. When asked whether he has any reasons to not proceed, Claudio turns on Hero, claiming she is not a virgin and has betrayed him. Leonato initially believes that Claudio must have been her bed-fellow yet Claudio rejects this, saying he has been the perfect gentleman. Don Pedro joins in with the attack and even her father, Leonato, is convinced, wishing that she was dead.

Claudio and Don Pedro leave and the Friar, believing Hero, devises a plan in which they pretend that Hero has died in order to allow time to clear her name. Leonato eventually agrees to this and Benedick agrees to keep it a secret. When alone, Benedick professes his love to Beatrice, yet she is more concerned with venting her anger towards Claudio; if he really loves her, she argues, then he will kill Claudio in Hero's name. Benedick refuses at first, yet realising that it will help to show his love for Beatrice, plans to seek out Claudio for a duel.

Scene 2

Borachio and Conrad are questioned by the watch while the Sexton takes notes. We hear that Don John has fled and Hero has 'died' – the prisoners are handcuffed and led away to Leonato. Dogberry finds the insults that he receives extremely comical, commenting that he wishes they had been written down!

© BADGER PUBLISHING

Act 5 Summary

Scene 1

Leonato discusses his feelings of shame about Hero with his brother, Antonio, who tries to calm him down. When Don Pedro and Claudio arrive, he turns his anger at them, resulting in the men being on the verge of a fight; Claudio shows no remorse for Hero's 'death' and Don Pedro refuses to listen to them.

Benedick arrives and is angry with Claudio and Don Pedro for what they have done to Hero; as a result, Benedick challenges Claudio to a duel which receives a dismissive response from the princes, who fail to take him seriously at first. Before he leaves, Benedick informs Don Pedro that his brother, Don John, has fled.

Dogberry arrives with the prisoner, Borachio, who confesses his sins and admits that he tricked the men into thinking Hero was with another man – the lady at the window was actually Margaret. Disgusted with themselves, Claudio and Don Pedro hear of Don John's guilt and realise that they have been responsible for Hero's 'death', promising to undertake any punishment that is decided upon. Leonato says they must inform the people of Messina of Hero's innocence, hang a mourning verse on her tomb; Claudio is then asked to marry Hero's cousin instead, to which he agrees. The criminals are taken away, whilst Leonato wishes to discover Margaret's involvement in the plot. Dogberry feels that his sense of importance has been increased through being referred to as "an ass".

Scene 2

Benedick arrives to see Beatrice with news that he has challenged Claudio to a duel. Before they meet, he attempts to write love poetry yet realises that it is not for him; when they do meet, there is still the banter and word play yet it has an affectionate tone – they are clearly in love and are not too stubborn to admit it, yet still maintain their vibrant personalities. Beatrice is pleased to hear that Claudio has been challenged and they are both delighted when official news of Hero's innocence is revealed.

MUCH ADO 2007
© BADGER PUBLISHING

Scene 3

Claudio and Don Pedro visit the 'monument' of Hero and ask for forgiveness – they promise to visit the monument every year.

Scene 4

The Friar comments that he has been proved right and Leonato is prepared to pardon Claudio and Don Pedro as well as forgiving Margaret's involvement. Benedick asks the friar about the possibility of being married to Beatrice. Before the service, Claudio mocks Benedick and he responds aggressively. When the bride arrives, Claudio discovers to his delight that the lady is actually Hero – the friar agrees to explain all later.

In the meantime, Benedick and Beatrice still have difficulty in admitting they are in love, yet their true feelings are revealed through the discovery of love letters they had written to each other; despite the jokes, Benedick still plans to marry Beatrice before they all go off for a celebration dance.

Chapter 3 - Key scenes, including explanation and glossary

Act 1, Scene 1 (1-39)

Outside Leonato's house. Enter LEONATO (Governor of Messina), his daughter HERO, his niece BEATRICE, and a MESSENGER.

LEONATO	I learn in this letter that Don Pedro of Aragon comes this night to Messina.	
MESSENGER	He is very near by this; he was not **three leagues** off when I left him.	
LEONATO	How many gentlemen have you lost in this **action**?	5
MESSENGER	But few of **any sort**, and none of name.	
LEONATO	A victory is twice itself when the achiever brings home full numbers. I find here that Don Pedro hath **bestowed much honour on** a young Florentine called Claudio.	
MESSENGER	Much deserved on his part and equally remembered by Don Pedro. **He hath borne himself beyond the promise of his age**, **doing in the figure of a lamb the feats of a lion**. He hath indeed better bettered expectation than you must expect of me to tell you how.	10
LEONATO	He hath an uncle here in Messina will be very much glad of it.	15
MESSENGER	I have already delivered him letters, and there appears much joy in him; even so much that joy could not show itself modest enough without a **badge of bitterness**.	
LEONATO	Did he break out into tears?	20
MESSENGER	In great measure.	
LEONATO	A kind overflow of kindness. There are no faces truer than those that are so washed. How much better is it to weep at joy than to joy at weeping!	
BEATRICE	I pray you, is **Signior Mountanto** returned from the wars, or no?	25
MESSENGER	I know none of that name, lady; there was none such in the army of any sort.	
LEONATO	What is he that you ask for, niece.	
HERO	My cousin means Signior Benedick of Padua.	30
MESSENGER	O, he's returned, and as pleasant as ever he was.	
BEATRICE	He set up his **bills** here in Messina, and **challenged Cupid at the flight**; and my uncle's fool, reading the challenge, subscribed for Cupid, and challenged him at the **bird-bolt**. I pray you, how many hath he killed and eaten in these wars? But how many hath he killed? For indeed I promised to eat all of his killing.	35
LEONATO	Faith, niece, you tax Signior Benedick too much; but he'll be meet with you, I doubt it not.	

MUCH ADO 2007

© BADGER PUBLISHING

Explanation

Leonato, the governor of Messina, is with his daughter, Hero, and niece, Beatrice, as they eagerly await the arrival of the princes who are returning victorious from a recent battle. When Leonato asks the messenger about the fatalities in the war, he comments "But few of any sort, and none of name." This immediately establishes the importance of class in the play and the rather snobby attitude the characters have towards the 'minor' characters and the lower classes. We discover that Don Pedro, the Prince of Aragon, has been praising the feats of the young Prince Claudio; this is in sharp contrast to the emotional weaknesses and shallow personality that we see Claudio exhibiting later in the play. The joy of victory has even brought tears to his uncle (who is never heard of again). Leonato comments that faces that are washed by tears are the most truthful; this reflects the dominant theme of appearance and reality in the play and the obsession with appearance and public display versus private meditation.

Beatrice's first words in the play are indicative of her vociferous personality: "Is Signior Mountanto returned from the wars, or no?" She is comparing Benedick to a fencing action – a thrust – which has a sexual innuendo and also sets up the intense verbal exchange that will dominate the play from now on. Moreover, it also introduces Benedick as a man who perhaps perceives himself as having great sexual prowess and a social climber. Beatrice reinforces this description through her comments that Benedick believes he is better at attracting ladies than Cupid. She also questions his ability as a soldier by claiming that she will eat all his killings. Leonato establishes the background of their relationship for the audience by saying that Benedick will get even with her when he arrives.

Glossary

three leagues – about nine miles

action – the recent war

any sort – any rank/any importance

bestowed much honour on – granted many favours to

He hath borne himself beyond the promise of his age –
his achievements are amazing considering how young he is

doing in the figure of a lamb the feats of a lion –
he has acted like a brave and hardened soldier in spite of his young age

badge of bitterness – his display of tears

Signior Mountanto – meaning 'to climb' and 'upward thrust' - Beatrice is referring to Benedick as a social climber (also sexual innuendo – to thrust)

bills – posters/advertisements

challenged Cupid at the flight – referring to Benedick claiming he could make more women fall in love with him than Cupid could (in Roman mythology, the god of love)

bird-bolt – a blunt arrow used to stun birds at a short distance

MESSENGER	He hath done good service, lady, in these wars.	40
BEATRICE	You had musty victual, and he hath holp to eat it. He is a very valiant trencher-man; he hath an excellent stomach.	
MESSENGER	And a good soldier too, lady.	
BEATRICE	And a good soldier to a lady. But what is he to a lord?	45
MESSENGER	A lord to a lord, a man to a man, stuffed with all honourable virtues.	
BEATRICE	It is so, indeed; he is no less than a **stuffed man**. But for the stuffing – well, we are all mortal.	
LEONATO	You must not, sir, mistake my niece. There is a kind of merry war **betwixt** Signior Benedick and her. They never meet but there's a **skirmish of wit** between them.	50
BEATRICE	Alas, he gets nothing by that. In our last conflict **four of his five wits** went halting off, and now is the whole man governed with one: so that if he have wit enough to keep himself warm, let him bear it for a difference between himself and his horse; for it is all the wealth that he hath left, to be known a **reasonable creature**. Who is his **companion** now? He hath every month a new sworn brother.	55 / 60
MESSENGER	Is't possible?	
BEATRICE	Very easily possible. **He wears his faith but as the fashion of his hat**: it ever changes with the next block.	
MESSENGER	I see, lady, the gentleman is **not in your books**.	
BEATRICE	No: an he were, I would burn my study. But, I pray you, who is his companion? Is there no young **squarer** now that will make a voyage with him to the devil?	65
MESSENGER	He is most in the company of the right noble Claudio.	
BEATRICE	O Lord, he will hang upon him like a disease. He is sooner caught than the **pestilence**, and the **taker** runs presently mad. God help the noble Claudio! **If he have caught the Benedick**, it will cost him a thousand pound ere 'a be cured.	70
MESSENGER	I will hold friends with you, lady.	
BEATRICE	Do, good friend.	75
LEONATO	*You* will never run mad, niece.	
BEATRICE	No, not till a hot January.	
MESSENGER	Don Pedro is approached.	

MUCH ADO 2007
© BADGER PUBLISHING

Explanation

The messenger innocently replies to Beatrice's verbal assault by commenting that Benedick has done good service in the wars; Beatrice uses food metaphors in a sarcastic way to further suggest that Benedick's apparent abilities as a soldier are in question. She admits that he is a good soldier "to a lady" which implies some hidden attraction on her part, yet she quickly reverts to type by using the pun of stuffing to suggest he is nothing more than a scarecrow or dummy. Leonato further explains the "merry war" and "skirmish of wit" that exists between Beatrice and Benedick; this helps to fire the audience's sense of anticipation before their meeting.

Beatrice continues to mock her rival, suggesting that he has lost four of his five wits and the one remaining cannot even put him above the status of a horse! Also, she implies that he is insincere and shallow, revealed by her comments that he has a "new sworn brother" every month. If he were in her "books", as the messenger comments, she would burn her study. It is interesting that Beatrice seems quite obsessed with Benedick, in spite of her ridicule, and insists on discovering who his new companion is. We hear of the Prince's imminent arrival.

Glossary

stuffed man – a scarecrow/dummy

betwixt - between

skirmish of wit – sharp and clever conversation

four of his five wits – the five wits were considered to be imagination, common sense, judgment, memory and fantasy

reasonable creature – Beatrice is referring to the capacity of reason which is supposed to distance ourselves from animals

companion – friend/colleague

He wears his faith but as the fashion of his hat –
Benedick easily changes his friends and never remains loyal to anyone

not in your books – not in favour with you

squarer – trouble-maker

pestilence – plague

taker – person who catches the plague

If he have caught the Benedick – Beatrice is punning on the theme of illness, suggesting that Claudio needs to rid himself of the "disease" that is Benedick

You **will never run mad** – Beatrice's negative attitude towards Benedick (and the opposite sex in general) will never change

Act 1, Scene 1 (79-123)

Enter DON PEDRO, CLAUDIO, BENEDICK, BALTHASAR, and DON JOHN the bastard (Don Pedro's half-brother).

DON PEDRO	Good Signior Leonato, are you come to meet your trouble? The fashion of the world is to avoid cost, and you **encounter** it.	80
LEONATO	Never came trouble to my house in the likeness of your Grace. For trouble being gone, comfort should remain; but when you depart from me sorrow **abides**, and happiness takes his leave.	85
DON PEDRO	You embrace your **charge** too willingly. (*Indicating HERO*) I think this is your daughter.	
LEONATO	Her mother hath many times told me so.	
BENEDICK	Were you in doubt, sir, that you asked her?	
LEONATO	Signior Benedick, no; for then were you a child.	90
DON PEDRO	**You have it full**, Benedick: we may guess by this what you are, being a man. **Truly, the lady fathers herself.** (*To HERO*) Be happy, lady; for you are like an honourable father.	
BENEDICK	If Signior Leonato be her father, she would not have his head on her shoulders for all Messina, as like him as she is.	95

DON PEDRO and LEONATO move aside to talk.

BEATRICE	I wonder that you will still be talking, Signior Benedick. Nobody **marks** you.	
BENEDICK	What, my dear **Lady Disdain**! Are you yet living?	100
BEATRICE	Is it possible disdain should die while she hath such **meet** food to feed it as Signior Benedick? Courtesy itself must **convert** to disdain, if you come in her presence.	
BENEDICK	Then is courtesy a **turncoat**. But it is certain I am loved of all ladies, only you excepted; and I would I could find in my heart that I had not a hard heart, for, truly, I love none.	105
BEATRICE	A dear happiness to women: they would else have been troubled with a **pernicious suitor**! I thank God and my cold blood, I am of your humour for that. I had rather hear my dog bark at a crow than a man swear he loves me.	110
BENEDICK	God keep your ladyship still in that mind! So some gentleman or other shall 'scape a **predestinate** scratched face.	115
BEATRICE	Scratching could not make it worse, and 'twere such a face as yours were.	
BENEDICK	Well, you are a rare **parrot-teacher**.	
BEATRICE	A bird of my tongue is better than a beast of yours.	
BENEDICK	**I would my horse had the speed of your tongue, and so good a continuer**. But keep your way, a' God's name. I have done.	120
BEATRICE	You always end with a **jade's trick**: I know you of old.	

MUCH ADO 2007

© BADGER PUBLISHING

Explanation

Don Pedro, Claudio, Benedick and Don John arrive with Balthasar – it is interesting that Don John is immediately described as a 'bastard' and therefore illegitimate; in Shakespeare's time, these characters were often presented as outsiders, villains with a jealous axe to grind, and we discover later than Don John is no exception. The exchange between the characters is overtly polite, courtly and good natured – in sharp contrast to the exchange between Benedick and Beatrice later in the scene. Don Pedro mentions Hero, Leonato's daughter, and Benedick's first words, implying that Hero's legitimacy may be in doubt, immediately set him up as the joker in the pack who has a mischievous side to him – very like Beatrice. Leonato's reply that he is sure because Benedick was only a child (and couldn't possibly be the father) reinforces Beatrice's view of him as a ladies' man.

Beatrice and Benedick finally meet, with the audience already anticipating an intense verbal exchange. Ironically, Beatrice's first words to Benedick are that no one notices him or is giving him attention, yet she is the one approaching him – this is a subtle sign of the love/hate relationship that will ensue between the couple. The food metaphor is extended through the exchange, with Beatrice commenting that her disdain (for him) will thrive when it has such suitable food to feast on. She also says that courtesy will turn to disdain if Benedick ever approaches it.

Benedick replies that courtesy must be a "turncoat" (ever changing) and that he is loved by all ladies, Beatrice excepted. He is determined that his hard heart will ensure that he will love no woman. In response, Beatrice claims that this statement will be met by joy from all women as they would not wish to be with such a destructive character as Benedick. On the topic of rejecting the opposite sex, they find agreement, with Beatrice commenting that she would rather hear a dog bark at a crow than a man profess his love. Benedick repeats the previous insults by suggesting that a scratched face would be the inevitable punishment of a man who would go near the lady. Rather than continue the clever verbal witticisms, Beatrice speaks plainly, saying that Benedick's face would not look any worse if it was scratched. Seeming tired of the banter, Benedick simply calls her a "parrot-teacher" – someone who copies his words. The final comment by Beatrice in this scene is dramatically significant, "I know you of old", as it implies a previous relationship between the two; in the other key scene, this theory is given further credibility – all of which may explain the "merry war" that exists between them.

Glossary

encounter – come to meet

abides – stays/remains

charge – heavy responsibility

You have it full – you have been told/corrected

Truly, the lady fathers herself – Hero looks like her father in appearance

marks – is paying attention to

Lady Disdain – Benedick is suggesting that Beatrice is full of contempt

meet – suitable – though also punning on the word 'meat' (food metaphor)

convert – change

turncoat - someone/thing that changes its loyalties

pernicious suitor – destructive/dangerous lover

predestinate – inevitable

parrot-teacher – someone who copies your words

I would my horse had the speed of your tongue, and so good a continuer -
I wish that my horse was as fast as your words and lasted as long

jade's trick – a tired and dangerous horse who refuses to finish
the race (the argument)

Act 2, Scene 1 (183-229)

Enter DON PEDRO, with LEONATO and HERO following.

DON PEDRO	*(To BENEDICK)* Now signior, where's the Count? Did you see him?
BENEDICK	**Troth**, my lord, I have played the part of Lady Fame. 185
	I found him here as **melancholy** as a **lodge in a warren**.
	I told him, and I think I told him true, that your Grace
	had got the good will of this young lady; and I offered
	him my company to a willow-tree, either to make him
	a garland, as being **forsaken**, or to bind him up a rod, as 190
	being worthy to be whipped.
DON PEDRO	To be whipped! What's his fault?
BENEDICK	The **flat transgression** of a schoolboy – who being
	overjoyed with finding a bird's nest, shows it his
	companion, and he steals it. 195
DON PEDRO	Wilt thou make a trust a transgression? The transgression
	is in the stealer.
BENEDICK	Yet it had not been amiss the rod had been made, and
	the garland too: for the garland he might have worn
	himself, **and the rod he might have bestowed on you**, 200
	who, as I take it, have stolen his bird's nest.
DON PEDRO	I will but teach them to sing, and **restore them to the**
	owner.
BENEDICK	If their singing answer your saying, by my faith you say
	honestly. 205
DON PEDRO	The Lady Beatrice hath a quarrel to you: the gentleman
	that danced with her told her she is much wronged by
	you.
BENEDICK	O, she misused me past the **endurance of a block**! An
	oak but with one green leaf on it would have answered 210
	her. **My very visor** began to assume life and scold with
	her. She told me, not thinking I had been myself, that I
	was the Prince's **jester**, that I was **duller than a great**
	thaw – huddling jest upon jest with such **impossible**
	conveyance upon me that I stood **like a man at a mark**, 215
	with a whole army shooting at me. She speaks **poniards**,
	and every word stabs. If her breath were as terrible as
	her **terminations**, there were no living near her: she
	would infect to the north star. I would not marry her,
	though she **were endowed with** all that Adam had left 220
	him **before he transgressed**. She would have made
	Hercules have turned spit, yea, and have cleft his club
	to make the fire too. Come, talk not of her. You shall find
	her the infernal **Até** in good apparel. I would to God
	some scholar would **conjure her**. For certainly, while 225
	she is here, a man may live as quiet in hell as in a
	sanctuary, and **people sin upon purpose** because they
	would go thither. So indeed, all disquiet, horror, and
	perturbation follows her.

MUCH ADO 2007

© BADGER PUBLISHING

Explanation

The masked ball. Just before this extract, the characters have been disguised and misunderstandings and conflicts have prevailed: Don John has told Claudio that Don Pedro has been trying to win Hero's affections for himself whilst Beatrice and Benedick have been exploiting their disguise to engage in exchanging insults.

It is clear that Benedick is also of the mind that Don Pedro is in love with Hero and explains that he offered Claudio two choices: a place to feel sad and depressed or to be whipped for the sin of being naïve in love, which is shown through him finding the bird's nest (Hero) and then showing it to his companion (Don Pedro), who steals it (the suggestion being that Don Pedro has wooed Hero for himself and betrayed Claudio). Don Pedro corrects Benedick's mistake and confirms that he has been acting on behalf of Claudio and will teach the bird (Hero) to sing (agree to marry) and return her to the owner (Claudio).

Don Pedro comments that Beatrice feels upset with Benedick and this receives an angry and emotional response from Benedick, who comments that she verbally abused him by saying he was dull and the "Prince's jester". He was made to feel that he was attacked by a dagger – Beatrice's words cut deep into him. Benedick continues the tirade by saying that everyone who is unlucky enough to be in her company will be infected and poisoned by her presence. Moreover, he would never marry her, even if she had the same attributes that God had bestowed upon Adam before he sinned (from the story of Adam and Eve). Benedick stays with the historical comparisons by suggesting that even Hercules (the strong man from Greek myth) would rather spend time in the kitchen, chopping up his great club for fire, than be with her. He also compares her to the goddess of vengeance and mischief, wishing that someone would send her to hell. On this theme, Benedick says that a man would enjoy a quieter life in hell than be on the world with Beatrice – it would be like being in a sanctuary; people would commit sins on earth to ensure they would escape Beatrice.

Glossary

Troth – indeed
melancholy – sad / depressed
lodge in a warren – a tiny hideaway
forsaken – abandoned / left alone
flat transgression – simple sin
overjoyed with finding a bird's nest – reference to Claudio falling in love with Hero
shows it his companion – refers to Claudio sharing his love for Hero with Don Pedro
and he steals it – reference to Don Pedro allegedly wooing Hero for himself
and the rod he might have bestowed on you – Claudio should whip Don Pedro himself
restore them to the owner – Don Pedro vows to return Hero to Claudio
endurance of a block – what a block of wood could stand (Beatrice's attack)
My very visor – my mask
jester – joker / fool
duller than a great thaw – more boring than watching snow melt
impossible conveyance – incredible flood of communication
like a man at a mark – he felt like he was about to be shot at when Beatrice abused him
poniard – dagger
terminations – her words / insults
were endowed with – possessed
before he transgressed – reference to when Adam disobeyed God
Hercules have turned spit – the great hero from Greek mythology would rather spend time in the kitchen than be with her
Até – reference to the God of vengeance and mischief
conjure her – send to hell
people sin upon purpose – people would sin intentionally in order to escape Beatrice and be sent to hell

Act 2, Scene 1 (230-274)

Enter CLAUDIO and BEATRICE.

DON PEDRO	Look, here she comes.	230
BENEDICK	Will your Grace command me any service to the world's end? I will go on the slightest errand now to the **Antipodes** that you can devise to send me on. I will fetch you a **tooth-picker** now from the furthest inch of Asia; bring you the length of **Prester John's** foot; fetch you a hair off the **great Cham's** beard; do you any embassage to the **Pigmies** – rather than hold three words' conference with this **harpy**. You have no employment for me?	235
DON PEDRO	None, but to desire your good company.	240
BENEDICK	O God, sir, here's a **dish** I love not. I cannot endure my **Lady Tongue**.	

Exit BENEDICK.

DON PEDRO	Come, lady, come. You have lost the heart of Signior Benedick.	
BEATRICE	Indeed, my lord, he lent it me awhile, and **I gave him use for it, a double heart for his single one**. Marry, once before he won it of me with false dice: therefore your Grace may well say I have lost it.	245
DON PEDRO	You have **put him down**, lady, you have put him down.	
BEATRICE	**So I would not he should do me**, my lord, lest I should prove **the mother of fools**. I have brought Count Claudio, whom you sent me to seek.	250
DON PEDRO	Why, how now, Count! Wherefore are you sad?	
CLAUDIO	Not sad, my lord.	
DON PEDRO	How then? Sick?	255
CLAUDIO	Neither, my lord.	
BEATRICE	The Count is neither sad, nor sick, nor merry, nor well; but **civil** count, civil as an orange, and something of that jealous complexion.	
DON PEDRO	I'faith, lady, I think your **blazon** to be true; though, I'll be sworn, if he be so, his conceit is false. Here, Claudio, I have wooed in thy name, and fair Hero is won. I have **broke with** her father, and **his good will obtained**. Name the day of marriage, and God give thee joy!	260
LEONATO	Count, take of me my daughter, and with her my fortunes. His Grace hath made the match and all grace say Amen to it!	265
BEATRICE	Speak, Count, 'tis your cue.	
CLAUDIO	**Silence is the perfectest herald of joy**. I were but little happy, if I could say how much. Lady, as you are mine, I am yours: I give away myself for you and **dote upon the exchange**.	270
BEATRICE	Speak, cousin – or, if you cannot, stop his mouth with a kiss, and let not him speak neither.	

MUCH ADO 2007

© BADGER PUBLISHING

Act 2, Scene 1 (230-274)
Explanation and Glossary

Explanation

Beatrice arrives with Claudio, which drives Benedick to get away quickly. He is so desperate that he says he is prepared to go to any extreme measure in order to get away from her and will even do a pointless task which includes going to the other side of the world for an errand and collecting a hair from the beard of the Emperor of China. This exaggerated language is used to demonstrate the hurt that Benedick is feeling yet Don Pedro fails to take him seriously and Benedick leaves hastily, saying he cannot cope with another ear bashing from Beatrice.

When Beatrice arrives, Don Pedro jokingly remarks that she has lost the heart of Benedick to which she agrees, revealing that she gave him her heart once before yet he misused it; this obviously implies a previous relationship that has existed between the two and one in which Beatrice's affections were not completely requited; this helps to explain the animosity that Beatrice feels towards Benedick, as well as her defensive attitude towards him – it is clear that she has a bigger axe to grind with him than vice-versa, and this revelation reinforces that suspicion. To add to this comment, Beatrice puns on Don Pedro's comment that she has put him down by referring to this as her being pregnant by Benedick which would mean the children would be fools.

Claudio is clearly distraught at the thought that he has lost Hero to Don Pedro who, he believes, has betrayed his trust. Don Pedro quickly corrects him and informs him that Hero has been "won" for him and her father, Leonato, has agreed to the marriage. All of this represents the theme of women being like property – a commodity that needs to be sold and agreed by the owner (the father). Hero's silence in this exchange is in sharp contrast to Beatrice's free-spirited nature. Claudio is shown to be rather shallow in the way his emotions switch from despair to joy in an instant – this has echoes of when he later believes the false accusation that Hero has been unfaithful.

Glossary

Antipodes – opposite side of the earth

tooth-picker – elaborate piece of jewellery from the East

Prester John – a Christian ruler who people believed may have been the King of Ethiopia

great Cham - Emperor of China

Pigmies – a race of small people

harpy – vulture who had the face and body of a woman

dish – meaning the grief that Beatrice will give out

Lady Tongue – referring to Beatrice's sharp words and cutting remarks

I gave him use for it, a double heart for his single one – Beatrice is implying there has been a previous relationship in which Benedick has let her down and played with her emotions

put him down – offended him

So I would not he should do me – Beatrice is choosing to interpret the "put him down" comment as Benedick making her pregnant

the mother of fools – if she had the children of Benedick they would all be fools

civil – meaning decent, though Beatrice plays on this word to suggest Seville, a Spanish city famous for oranges

blazon – a coat of arms described

broke with – discussed

his good will obtained – he (Leonato) has agreed

Silence is the perfectest herald of joy – my silence is a sign of my happiness

dote upon the exchange – overwhelmed that we should be together

MUCH ADO 2007
© BADGER PUBLISHING

Act 2, Scene 1 (275-310)

DON PEDRO	In faith, lady, you have a merry heart.	275
BEATRICE	Yea, my lord; I thank it, poor fool, it keeps on **the windy side of care**. My cousin tells him in his ear that he is in her heart.	
CLAUDIO	And so she doth, cousin.	
BEATRICE	**Good Lord, for alliance! Thus goes everyone to the world but I, and I am sunburnt**. I may sit in a corner and cry 'Heigh-ho for a husband!'	280
DON PEDRO	Lady Beatrice, I will get you one.	
BEATRICE	I would rather have one of your father's getting. Hath your Grace ne'er a brother like you? Your father got excellent husbands, if a maid could come by them.	285
DON PEDRO	Will you have *me*, lady?	
BEATRICE	No, my lord, unless I might have another for working-days. Your Grace is too costly to wear every day. But I beseech your Grace, pardon me: I was born to speak all **mirth and no matter**.	290
DON PEDRO	Your silence most offends me, and to be merry best becomes you; for, out of question, you were born in a merry hour.	
BEATRICE	No, sure, my lord, my mother cried. But then **there was a star danced, and under that was I born**. Cousins, God give you joy!	295
LEONATO	Niece, will you look to those things I told you of?	
BEATRICE	I cry you mercy, uncle. (*To DON PEDRO*) By your Grace's pardon.	300

Exit BEATRICE.

DON PEDRO	By my troth, a pleasant-spirited lady.	
LEONATO	There's little of the melancholy element in her, my lord. She is never sad but when she sleeps, and not ever sad then: for I have heard my daughter say, she hath often dreamt of unhappiness and waked herself with laughing.	305
DON PEDRO	She cannot endure to hear tell of a husband.	
LEONATO	O, by no means. She mocks all her wooers out of suit.	
DON PEDRO	She were an excellent wife for Benedick.	
LEONATO	O Lord, my lord, if they were but a week married, they would talk themselves mad.	310

MUCH ADO 2007

© BADGER PUBLISHING

Act 2, Scene 1 (275-310)
Explanation and Glossary

Explanation

Don Pedro and Beatrice again discuss marriage, with Beatrice implying that she feels slightly left out; this gets a half-serious/half-joking wedding proposal from Don Pedro, which she declines, explaining that he would be too costly and demanding and she should not be taken too seriously. When she exits, Don Pedro and Leonato discuss the high spirited Beatrice, revealing that there is little melancholy (sadness) in her - in fact she only dreams of it before waking herself up with laughing! Don Pedro says she would be an excellent wife for Benedick though Leonato disagrees, saying they would drive themselves mad if they were ever together.

Glossary

the windy side of care – Beatrice is referring to her vibrant nature which helps her overcome and combat worry and stress

Good lord for alliance! Thus goes every one to the world but I, and I am sunburnt - Everyone is getting married but me yet I am obviously out of fashion

mirth and no matter – nonsense

there was a star danced, and under that was I born – the influence of the star gave Beatrice her happy, cheerful personality

MUCH ADO 2007
© BADGER PUBLISHING

Act 2, Scene 1 (311-end)

DON PEDRO	Count Claudio, when mean you to go to church?
CLAUDIO	Tomorrow, my lord. **Time goes on crutches**, till love have all his rites.
LEONATO	Not till Monday, my dear son, which is hence a just seven-night – and a time too brief, too, to have all things answer my mind. 315
DON PEDRO	**Come, you shake the head at so long a breathing** – but I warrant thee, Claudio, the time shall not go dully by us. I will **in the interim** undertake one of **Hercules' labours** – which is, to bring Signior Benedick and the 320 Lady Beatrice into a mountain of affection, the one with the other. **I would fain have it a match**; and I doubt not but to fashion it, if you three will but **minister such assistance** as I shall give you direction.
LEONATO	My lord, I am for you, though it cost me ten nights' 325 watchings.
CLAUDIO	And I, my lord.
DON PEDRO	And you too, gentle Hero?
HERO	I will do any **modest office**, my lord, to help my cousin to a good husband. 330
DON PEDRO	And Benedick is not the unhopefullest husband that I know. Thus far can I praise him: he is of a noble strain, of approved **valour** and confirmed honesty. I will teach you how to humour your cousin, that she shall fall in love with Benedick. And I, with your two helps, will so 335 **practise** on Benedick that, in despite of his quick wit and his queasy stomach, he shall fall in love with Beatrice. If we can do this, **Cupid is no longer an archer: his glory shall be ours**, for we are the only love-gods. Go in with me, and I will tell you my drift. 340

Exeunt.

Explanation

Claudio wishes to marry Hero the following day yet Leonato says he needs more time to have things properly prepared. It also gives them a chance to try and trick Benedick and Beatrice into falling in love with each other. Don Pedro lists the good qualities of Benedick whilst Hero agrees to do what she can to help her cousin "to a good husband". Claudio and Leonato also agree to help in the hope of bringing them together. Don Pedro comments that, if they succeed, then they will rival Cupid as "love-gods".

Glossary

Time goes on crutches – time will last forever until we are married

Come, you shake the head at so long a breathing – Don Pedro notices that Claudio is despondent at having to wait a week to be married and tells him not to worry

in the interim – in the meantime

Hercules' labours – referring to the strong Greek hero who had to carry out seemingly impossible challenges

I would fain have it a match – I want them to be together in love

minister such assistance – give me what help (I request), i.e. do what I ask

modest office – what I can do

valour – bravery

practise – work on (deceive him of Beatrice's affections)

Cupid is no longer an archer: his glory shall be ours – we will be the match-makers

MUCH ADO 2007
© BADGER PUBLISHING

Chapter 4
Exploring the key scenes
50 probing questions with support

Act 1, Scene 1 (1-123)

The following questions have been designed to test your understanding of Act 1, Scene 1 and will allow you to demonstrate your analytical skills. You will notice that most questions demand that you refer to the actual scene and use examples to justify your point of view.

In the exam, you will be assessed on your ability to:
- Focus on the question.
- Use well chosen references to justify points made.
- Show clear understanding of Shakespeare's use of language and the impact on the audience.

Remember to write about this play as a piece of theatre; therefore you need to constantly refer to how the writer (Shakespeare) has used the characters and events to communicate his ideas to the audience (not reader). In order to achieve a Level 5 and above in your exam, you will need to ensure that you take the 3 steps in the table below:

Example question:
What does the audience learn about Beatrice's character from this extract?

Steps	Achieving Level 5+	Example
1	Focus on the question.	*Beatrice is revealed as being confident, brash and antagonistic.*
2	Well chosen references used to justify point made.	*"Is Signior Mountanto returned from the wars, or no?"*
3	Clear understanding of Shakespeare's use of language and the impact on the audience.	*Shakespeare uses this phrase "Mountanto" in two ways: firstly, it is a fencing reference, which could be an example of Beatrice mocking Benedick for his supposed fighting qualities; also, it could be used to refer to sexual thrust which suggests that Benedick fancies himself somewhat and Beatrice may have previous knowledge of this. The Shakesperian audience would feel surprised to see a woman holding court in the high office of Messina as, traditionally, women of the era (Hero is an embodiment of this) would reserve their own thoughts, allowing men to dominate proceedings.*

Exploring the key scenes
Act 1, Scene 1 (1-123)

You will notice that the following questions require far more than simply comprehension - you will need to demonstrate your awareness of the language used whilst ensuring that you use evidence carefully to justify your points. It is advisable to get into the habit of responding to *Much Ado about Nothing* in this way as it is what the examiner will be expecting when marking your exam.

1) What does the audience discover about Claudio from this extract?

2) How is this description of Claudio in sharp contrast to the man we meet later in the play? (use examples to justify points)

3) When the messenger comments that no one of importance died in the wars, what does that tell the audience about the importance of status and class to the characters and Leonato in particular?

4) How is the theme of appearance and reality explored in lines 22-24? What is ironic about Leonato's comments here? (refer to other significant events in the play)

5) Explain what Beatrice means when she says that Benedick challenged Cupid.

6) When Beatrice comments that she is happy to eat all of his killings, Shakespeare is using hyperbole (exaggeration) for dramatic effect. Why do you think she makes such a claim?

7) How does Leonato react to Beatrice's comments? What does he suggest will occur when Benedick arrives?

8) How does Beatrice pun on the words to/too?

9)   The metaphor of eating becomes extended when Beatrice and the messenger discuss 'stuffing'. How do they use this phrase and what effect is created?

10)   What does Leonato mean by a "merry war"?

11)   Beatrice continues to insult Benedick in his absence. Why does he so desperately need his one remaining wit, according to her?

12)   What is Beatrice suggesting about Benedick when she says that he has a "new sworn brother" every month?

13)   Beatrice insists on discovering who Benedick's companion is. What might this suggest about her deeply held thoughts towards him?

14)   How does Beatrice use the comparison of a "disease" when commenting on Claudio's relationship with Benedick?

15)   Don Pedro and Leonato enjoy a light-hearted debate when they first meet. What mood is created by their initial exchange?

16)   What is significant about Hero's silence throughout this whole scene? How is this in sharp contrast to her cousin, Beatrice?

17)   What do you think Shakespeare wanted his audience to consider about the roles of women in high society?

18)   How are Benedick's first words indicative of his character?

19)   What is ironic about Beatrice's first words to Benedick?

20) How do Benedick and Beatrice use the words "courtesy" and "disdain"?

21) What do these two rivals actually agree on?

22) Where is alliteration used by Benedick? What effect does it create on the audience?

23) How does the pace of the scene change with the argument between Benedick and Beatrice?

24) How do the characters use the following creatures to describe their thoughts and feelings?

- Dog
- Crow
- Parrot
- Bird
- Horse

25) From this opening scene, what impression does the audience get of:

- Messina
- Benedick and Beatrice
- The differing attitudes that are held towards love and marriage

Exploring the key scenes
Act 2, Scene 1 (183-end)

The following questions have been designed to test your understanding of Act 2, Scene 1 and will allow you to demonstrate your analytical skills. You will notice that most questions demand that you refer to the actual scene and use examples to justify your point of view.

In the exam, you will be assessed on your ability to:
- Focus on the question.
- Use well chosen references to justify points made.
- Show clear understanding of Shakespeare's use of language and the impact on the audience.

Remember to write about this play as a piece of theatre; therefore you need to constantly refer to how the writer (Shakespeare) has used the characters and events to communicate his ideas to the audience (not reader). In order to achieve a Level 5 and above in your exam, you will need to ensure that you take the 3 steps in the table below:

Example question:
What does the audience learn about the differing attitudes to love and marriage from this scene?

Steps	Achieving Level 5+	Example
1	Focus on the question.	*There is great contrast between Shakespeare's presentation of love and marriage in this scene; from the antagonistic and free-spirited Beatrice to the obedient and dutiful daughter who wishes to please her father above all else. Beatrice seems defensive and dismissive of the prospect of a husband, shown by her wry comment:*
2	Well chosen references used to justify point made.	*"I may sit in a corner and cry 'Heigh-ho for a husband!'"*
3	Clear understanding of Shakespeare's use of language and the impact on the audience.	*In contrast, Hero remains silent throughout, except when prompted about a different matter. Shakespeare begins to reveal a softening in Beatrice's attitude to marriage, demonstrated through this somewhat melancholy comment; perhaps the imminent wedding of Hero and Claudio has left her feeling lonely, especially after Benedick quickly disappeared on her arrival. Shakespeare wants his audience to consider the rights of women within a marriage; it is noticeable that Beatrice is the far more engaging character and she has the free spirit that Hero lacks; this may reflect Shakespeare's critical stance on the traditional courtship which seems to be without integrity.*

MUCH ADO 2007
© BADGER PUBLISHING

Exploring the key scenes
Act 2, Scene 1 (183-end)

You will notice that the following questions require far more than simply comprehension - you will need to demonstrate your awareness of the language used whilst ensuring that you use evidence carefully to justify your points. It is advisable to get into the habit of responding to *Much Ado about Nothing* in this way as it is what the examiner will be expecting when marking your exam.

1)   What significant misunderstanding has occurred before this scene?

2)   How has this misunderstanding contributed to the events of this scene?

3)   What is the simile that Benedick uses when discussing Claudio? What does that reveal about his state of mind?

4)   Benedick believes that Don Pedro has wooed Hero for himself and has seen his friend Claudio devastated by this 'news'. Explain why he has a mocking attitude towards the whole event.

5)   When Benedick and Don Pedro speak of the "bird's nest", what are they referring to?

6)   How is Hero described as a commodity? (someone's goods to be owned)

7)   What does this description of Hero reveal about Shakespeare's criticism of women's roles in high society?

8)   What are the insults that Benedick is so upset about? Why might these hit a nerve with Benedick? (consider his personality and the opinion he wants people to have about him)

9) How does Benedick use the weapons of guns and daggers to reveal his thoughts and feelings?

10) Shakespeare uses references to religion and the Greek myths in Benedick's speech. Using the table below, comment on what purpose they serve. (use the glossary sections from the key scenes for further explanation)

	Reference from the text	Why it's being used
Adam and Eve		
Hercules		
Até		

11) How are the following language devices used by Shakespeare to increase the impact of Benedick's complaint?

	Reference from the text	How this increases the impact of Benedick's speech
Simile		
Metaphor		
Personification		
Alliteration		
Hyperbole (exaggeration)		

MUCH ADO 2007
© BADGER PUBLISHING

12) How does Benedick react to Beatrice's arrival?

13) Benedick exaggerates greatly when seeing Beatrice arrive. Comment on why Benedick says he is prepared to do the following tasks for Don Pedro.

   - Go on a slight errand to the Antipodes.
   - Fetch a tooth-picker from Asia.
   - Bring the length of Prester John's foot.
   - Fetch a hair from the great Cham's beard.
   - Do any embassage to the Pigmies.

14) The use of food imagery is evident again in this scene. Find the quote which demonstrates it and explain its purpose.

15) How do we get the impression that Beatrice and Benedick have been together (romantically) before?

16) a) What is suggested about Benedick's previous treatment of Beatrice?
    b) How might this explain Beatrice's attitude towards him?

17) How is Claudio shown to be oversensitive and fickle in this scene?

18) a) What is significant about Hero's silence in this scene?
    b) How does she compare with her cousin?

19) What hints do the audience get that Beatrice may be secretly sad about being without a husband?

20) When Beatrice leaves, what do we learn about her character from Leonato, Don Pedro and Claudio?

21) Why do you feel that Leonato wants to wait a week before allowing the marriage of his daughter to Claudio?

22) What is the plan that Don Pedro devises?

23) Why would the audience feel a sense of great anticipation at the proposed match-making and deception that will ensue?

24) Compare the attitude towards love and marriage that exist between Benedick and Beatrice and Claudio and Hero.

25) From this scene, what does the audience learn about:

  • Claudio
  • The relationship between Hero and her father
  • Leonato
  • Beatrice

Chapter 5
Explaining the assessment focuses

As mentioned in the introduction, students will be asked a question based on one of the 4 assessment focuses chosen for the Shakespeare reading paper.

These are:

- Motivation and behaviour

- Ideas, themes and issues

- The language of the text

- The text in performance

It is important that students are aware of what these areas actually mean, and how to apply them to the actual text. In this way they should feel well-equipped to tackle whatever question comes their way.

Over the next few pages are a list of prompts that students can use when making notes on the key scenes (Chapter 6). The list of prompts is quite extensive and attempts to cover all areas of the key scenes; therefore, students will not be able to respond to each prompt for each section from the key scenes and will need guidance as to which prompts will be most pertinent to their note-making.

Motivation and behaviour

- What are the feelings of the characters during this scene?

- What makes them act in this particular way?

- What events have influenced them before this scene?

- Which characters have contributed to their behaviour in this scene?

- How are their motivations similar/different to those around them?

- Are their actions in this scene typical of them or out of character?

- How does Shakespeare reveal their motivations and behaviour?

- How do the other characters react to their actions?

- What impact do their actions in this scene have on the rest of the play?

- How would the audience react to their motivation and behaviour?

Ideas, themes and issues

Which themes feature in the extracts?

- Betrayal
- Control
- Marriage
- Relationships
- Obedience
- Tradition
- Class
- Deception
- Appearance and reality
- Conflict between old and young
- Men and women

How are the themes presented to the audience?

- Through the character's actions
- Their words
- Their body language
- Stage directions
- What other characters say about them

MUCH ADO 2007
© BADGER PUBLISHING

The language of the text

- Are there any particular language devices used?

    - soliloquy
    - symbolism
    - alliteration
    - rhyming couplets
    - varied line length
    - punctuation used for dramatic effect
    - hyperbole (exaggeration)
    - similes / metaphors / personification
    - rhythm variety
    - verse / prose

- What is the effect of the language on the audience? What mood is created?

    - tense atmosphere
    - increased pace
    - darken/lighten the mood

- How is the language used by the characters reflective of their personalities?

- Is their choice of words in keeping with their motives and behaviour?

- How do the characters disguise their true thoughts and feelings through their clever use of language?

- How would the audience react to the characters' use of language in the set scenes?

MUCH ADO 2007
© BADGER PUBLISHING

Text in performance

The question of how to direct the scenes is one that many students and teachers fear the most; partly because they see it as solely a drama-based question, and it is often difficult for many students to visualise the text and know the vocabulary that should be used within a dramatic and theatrical setting. The type of questions related to this theme can be categorised into the following:

- What advice would you give to an actor playing this character?

- How would you direct these scenes?

Remember to explain how your decisions as a director would help to communicate the following to a Shakespearian audience:

- the personality, behaviour and the inner relationships of the characters
- the atmosphere and mood of the scene
- the themes that are most evident in the scene

Atmosphere
How could the following be used to create the desired atmosphere?

- the organisation of the stage
- props; lighting; spot lights; fog; music/sound effects
- use of levels

Characterisation
How would you communicate the relationships between the characters as well as their individual feelings and actions?

- costume
- tone of voice; body language
- position and movement of characters
- emphasis of key words and phrases

Advice to the actor(s)
Consider how they should communicate their feelings to:

- themselves
- the other characters
- the audience

How to make notes using the assessment focuses

In Chapter 6, students are given the task of making comments on the key scenes in relation to the assessment focuses (using the prompts detailed in this chapter). To support this process, the opening section of each key scene has been completed here - which could be used to model with students how to respond in a concise, focused way.

Obviously, this is a subjective view – you may wish to model the responses with students as a shared writing activity. It may be an idea to photocopy the key scene and assessment focus response table onto an A3 sheet as students would benefit from having the key directly in front of them when responding, rather than flicking through the scenes in a different section which may lose their focus!

For example:

Act 1, Scene 1 (1-39)

Outside Leonato's house. Enter LEONATO (Governor of Messina), his daughter HERO, his niece BEATRICE, and a MESSENGER.

LEONATO	I learn in this letter that Don Pedro of Aragon comes this night to Messina.	
MESSENGER	He is very near by this; he was not three leagues off when I left him.	
LEONATO	How many gentlemen have you lost in this action?	5
MESSENGER	But few of any sort, and none of name.	
LEONATO	A victory is twice itself when the achiever brings home full numbers. I find here that Don Pedro hath bestowed much honour on a young Florentine called Claudio.	
MESSENGER	Much deserved on his part and equally remembered by Don Pedro. He hath borne himself beyond the promise of his age, doing in the figure of a lamb the feats of a lion. He hath indeed better bettered expectation than you must expect of me to tell you how.	10
LEONATO	He hath an uncle here in Messina will be very much glad of it.	15
MESSENGER	I have already delivered him letters, and there appears much joy in him; even so much that joy could not show itself modest enough without a badge of bitterness.	
LEONATO	Did he break out into tears?	20
MESSENGER	In great measure.	
LEONATO	A kind overflow of kindness. There are no faces truer than those that are so washed. How much better is it to weep at joy than to joy at weeping!	
BEATRICE	I pray you, is Signior Mountanto returned from the wars, or no?	25
MESSENGER	I know none of that name, lady; there was none such in the army of any sort.	
LEONATO	What is he that you ask for, niece.	
HERO	My cousin means Signior Benedick of Padua.	30
MESSENGER	O, he's returned, and as pleasant as ever he was.	
BEATRICE	He set up his bills here in Messina, and challenged Cupid at the flight; and my uncle's fool, reading the challenge, subscribed for Cupid, and challenged him at the bird-bolt. I pray you, how many hath he killed and eaten in these wars? But how many hath he killed? For indeed I promised to eat all of his killing.	35
LEONATO	Faith, niece, you tax Signior Benedick too much; but he'll be meet with you, I doubt it not.	

Reproduced with permission from the Longman School Shakespeare edition© Pearson Education Ltd (2004)

Responding to the assessment focuses
Act 1, Scene 1 (1-39)

Assessment focus and prompts	Student response
Motivation and behaviour What are the characters feeling? Why? Who influences them? Are their actions typical of them? How do the other characters react to them? What impact do their actions in this scene have on the rest of the play? How would the audience react to them?	
Ideas, themes and issues Which themes feature in the extracts? How are the themes presented to the audience? What issues might Shakespeare want his audience to think about?	
The language of the text What language devices are used? What is the effect of the language on the audience? How is punctuation used for dramatic effect? What mood is created? How is the language used by the characters reflective of their personalities?	
Text in performance *Atmosphere* - How would you create it? stage / lighting / colour / spotlights / fog / music / effects / levels *Characterisation* - Position / Movement / Costume / Tone of voice / Body language / Emphasis of key words *Advice to the actors* - How should they communicate to themselves / the other characters / the audience?	

Exemplar responses to each assessment focus
Act 1, Scene 1 (1-39)

Assessment focus and prompts	Exemplar response
Motivation and behaviour What are the characters feeling? Why? Who influences them? Are their actions typical of them? How do the other characters react to them? What impact do their actions in this scene have on the rest of the play? How would the audience react to them?	*Shakespeare wants his audience to quickly identify with the main characters. Leonato's overly formal and courtly tone is presented here as is a strong belief in the family name/honour which motivates many of his actions; this is revealed through his comment that the victory in the war was twice itself because "none of name" were killed. We also learn that Claudio and Don Pedro are close allies – a friendship that contributes to them jointly accusing Hero of betrayal later in the play. It's interesting that Claudio is described as brave and noble in battle, yet this is in sharp contrast to his rather pathetic and shallow personality that we learn of later. Beatrice's motivation in this early exchange is clear: she wishes to present herself as a woman of conviction, independence and free spirited, as well as establishing her public opinion of Benedick; in terms of the wider picture, it is clear that this aggressive stance is mostly a sign of self-preservation and a response to being rejected by Benedick in the past.*
Ideas, themes and issues Which themes feature in the extracts? How are the themes presented to the audience? What issues might Shakespeare want his audience to think about?	*The issue of class and the hierarchical nature of Messina is ironically presented here through Leonato being established as being ignorant to the lower-classes (to his cost later in the play when he ignores Dogberry's revelations about Hero's accusers). The dominant themes of appearance and reality are introduced here through the words of Leonato, who comments that faces washed by tears are the most true; Shakespeare has included this to create dramatic irony as it is the unkempt characters (the watchers) who actually reveal the truth (about Hero's innocence) later in the play. A key issue in the whole play is the conflict between men and women and the attitude the characters have towards love and marriage. Beatrice quickly explores this theme through her jibing of Benedick and rejection of his belief that he is better at attracting a mate than Cupid.*

© BADGER PUBLISHING

Exemplar responses to each assessment focus
Act 1, Scene 1 (1-39)

Assessment focus and prompts	Exemplar response
The language of the text What language devices are used? What is the effect of the language on the audience? How is punctuation used for dramatic effect? What mood is created? How is the language used by the characters reflective of their personalities?	*The formal language and politeness of the opening exchange quickly establishes the general upbeat mood, especially after the recent battle victorys. The relaxed use of prose, rather than Shakespeare's more frequent use of verse, reinforces the sedate and gentle mood. Animal imagery is used to describe the characteristics of Claudio and it is interesting that the lion was used to describe him in battle yet he seems to possess (later in the play) more feeble and weak characteristics that you would associate with a lamb. The use of a fencing and sexual metaphor ("Signior Mountanto") by Beatrice when describing Benedick has two functions: it reveals her contempt for Benedick as well as establishing Benedick as a ladies' man. Food imagery is used frequently in this play and is introduced by Beatrice who claims she will eat all of Benedick's killings (a soldiers' boast in battle) which shows she questions his ability as a soldier and a man. It is important to see how the pace and tone of the scene changes dramatically on Beatrice's arrival – the courtly exchange and slow pace is quickened up by her free-spirited and energetic arrival.*
Text in performance *Atmosphere* - How would you create it? stage / lighting / colour / spotlights / fog / music / effects / levels *Characterisation* - position / movement / costume / tone of voice / body language / emphasis of key words *Advice to the actors* - How should they communicate to themselves / the other characters / the audience?	*The key dramatic features from this extract would be to use the stage in a way that reflects the civilized setting of Messina as well as the joyous mood of celebration that permeates the scene; Leonato's status as the governor should be established through the use of costume / stage levels and the calm environment could be created by sensual music of the time as well as soft lighting to establish the care-free attitude that exists. All of these aspects need to alter when Beatrice enters the action – her witty yet vindictive comments should be presented with disdain and sarcasm - the mood altering through a more intense use of light, a quickening of the music. Beatrice should come across as confident and brash with her Uncle Leonato and demonstrate that she is not intimidated by the male dominated society – unlike her cousin, Hero.*

MUCH ADO 2007
© BADGER PUBLISHING

Exemplar responses to each assessment focus
Act 2, Scene 1 (183-229)

Assessment focus and prompts	Student response
Motivation and behaviour What are the characters feeling? Why? Who influences them? Are their actions typical of them? How do the other characters react to them? What impact do their actions in this scene have on the rest of the play? How would the audience react to them?	*As this scene is concerned with misunderstandings and confusion, the characters are motivated by the need to explain their intentions and correct misunderstandings. Benedick clearly feels that Don Pedro has been wooing Hero for himself yet maintains his sense of wit and use of word play to jokingly confront his friend over this. His comments about the devastated Claudio also have a ring of insincerity and mild scorn. Don Pedro corrects the mistake and seems content within himself to be the match-maker. Benedick's dramatic response to Beatrice's insults shows his sensitive side (despite his macho mask) as well as how much he is concerned with her opinion of him; it is this concern that Don Pedro and Claudio exploit.*
Ideas, themes and issues Which themes feature in the extracts? How are the themes presented to the audience? What issues might Shakespeare want his audience to think about?	*The theme of deception as well as appearance and reality is explored here during the aftermath of the masked ball, where the impression that Don Pedro was wooing Hero for himself has the impact of devastating the gullible Claudio. Shakespeare uses the masked ball to allow the characters to reveal their true thoughts as well as to provide dramatic tension and conflict. The characters' attitude to love and marriage is also expressed here through the very fact that Don Pedro has been trying to 'win' the heart of Hero for Claudio – this rather sexist and over-courtly system is in sharp contrast to the way that Beatrice and Benedick communicate. Through Benedick's expression of dismay and his verbal attack on Beatrice, the audience learn that Beatrice is able to touch a nerve in Benedick and reach his heart, albeit for pain rather than pleasure; Shakespeare is further creating such an apparent divide between these characters so that the planned entrapment will be all the more interesting to observe.*

© BADGER PUBLISHING

Exemplar responses to each assessment focus
Act 2, Scene 1 (183-239)

Assessment focus and prompts	Student response
The language of the text What language devices are used? What is the effect of the language on the audience? How is punctuation used for dramatic effect? What mood is created? How is the language used by the characters reflective of their personalities?	*Benedick uses the extended metaphor of a wood to describe the forlorn Claudio, who has been seemingly betrayed by Don Pedro and lost the heart of Hero. This naturalist imagery continues with Benedick comparing the finding of love with a "bird's nest" which Don Pedro has stolen. Shakespeare wants his audience to consider how women were often treated as property that was owned (as in the example of Leonato controlling all of Hero's decisions). Benedick describes his feelings for Beatrice using a vast array of images, using personification "She speaks poniards" and hyperbole (exaggeration) "she would infect to the north star". This reveals Benedick's overactive imagination as well as his genuine upset at the way Beatrice has treated him. Shakespeare frequently uses references to religion (Adam and Eve) and Greek mythology (infernal Até / Hercules) to provide a greater dramatic edge and force to the character's language.*
Text in performance *Atmosphere* - How would you create it? stage / lighting / colour / spotlights / fog / music / effects / levels *Characterisation* - position / movement / costume / tone of voice / body language / emphasis of key words *Advice to the actors* - How should they communicate to themselves / the other characters / the audience?	*The first stage direction of this scene 'Enter DON PEDRO, with LEONATO and HERO following' is particularly significant as Hero falls into the category of obedient and submissive female whose decisions are made by her father. It should be demonstrated that Hero is indeed following her father in every way. When Benedick is commenting on the melancholy of Claudio, it should be made clear that he is insincere and rather agitated with the love-struck lord. Benedick should act out the whipping section with glee and generally mimic the actions of Claudio, revealing his (seemingly) dismissive attitude towards love and marriage. When matters turn to Beatrice's previous condemnation of him, Benedick should become visibly animated and upset, whispering the repeated insults into Don Pedro's ear for fear of public shame. The melodramatic nature of Benedick should come to the fore here, with him acting out the 'stabbing' and being 'shot at by the army'. In return, Don Pedro should be in fits of laughter at hearing this as he is much amused by their "merry war". Darkened lighting should be focused on Benedick in contrast to the mellow colours of the characters around him, which will help to communicate his anger. Benedick's body language and facial expression should be more shock than despair due to the damage done to his ego.*

Chapter 6
Responding to the assessment focuses
Student worksheets

The purpose of this chapter is to revisit the key scenes in relation to the assessment focuses for reading. This task should only be attempted when students are already very familiar with the scenes themselves and are therefore able to apply their knowledge within the context of the assessment focuses.

You will find the key scenes recopied here with a table alongside each section for students to make notes related to each of the assessment focuses for reading. There is only a limited space for students to respond which was designed to help them clarify and concentrate their thoughts in a concise way. Subsequently, it will be important to ensure that students are familiar with the skills of responding concisely.

Each response should be:

- concise
- relevant
- appropriate for the purpose of the task
- related directly to the assessment focuses in that particular key scene
- legible for later use as a revision tool

It is advisable to copy the extract and response table side by side on A3 paper so that students can directly relate their thoughts on the relevant extracts. For example:

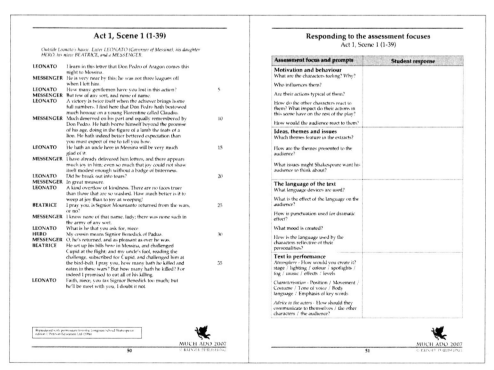

MUCH ADO 2007

Act 1, Scene 1 (1-39)

Outside Leonato's house. Enter LEONATO (Governor of Messina), his daughter HERO, his niece BEATRICE, and a MESSENGER.

LEONATO	I learn in this letter that Don Pedro of Aragon comes this night to Messina.	
MESSENGER	He is very near by this; he was not three leagues off when I left him.	
LEONATO	How many gentlemen have you lost in this action?	5
MESSENGER	But few of any sort, and none of name.	
LEONATO	A victory is twice itself when the achiever brings home full numbers. I find here that Don Pedro hath bestowed much honour on a young Florentine called Claudio.	
MESSENGER	Much deserved on his part and equally remembered by Don Pedro. He hath borne himself beyond the promise of his age, doing in the figure of a lamb the feats of a lion. He hath indeed better bettered expectation than you must expect of me to tell you how.	10
LEONATO	He hath an uncle here in Messina will be very much glad of it.	15
MESSENGER	I have already delivered him letters, and there appears much joy in him; even so much that joy could not show itself modest enough without a badge of bitterness.	
LEONATO	Did he break out into tears?	20
MESSENGER	In great measure.	
LEONATO	A kind overflow of kindness. There are no faces truer than those that are so washed. How much better is it to weep at joy than to joy at weeping!	
BEATRICE	I pray you, is Signior Mountanto returned from the wars, or no?	25
MESSENGER	I know none of that name, lady; there was none such in the army of any sort.	
LEONATO	What is he that you ask for, niece.	
HERO	My cousin means Signior Benedick of Padua.	30
MESSENGER	O, he's returned, and as pleasant as ever he was.	
BEATRICE	He set up his bills here in Messina, and challenged Cupid at the flight; and my uncle's fool, reading the challenge, subscribed for Cupid, and challenged him at the bird-bolt. I pray you, how many hath he killed and eaten in these wars? But how many hath he killed? For indeed I promised to eat all of his killing.	35
LEONATO	Faith, niece, you tax Signior Benedick too much; but he'll be meet with you, I doubt it not.	

MUCH ADO 2007

© BADGER PUBLISHING

Responding to the assessment focuses
Act 1, Scene 1 (1-39)

Assessment focus and prompts	Student response
Motivation and behaviour What are the characters feeling? Why? Who influences them? Are their actions typical of them? How do the other characters react to them? What impact do their actions in this scene have on the rest of the play? How would the audience react to them?	
Ideas, themes and issues Which themes feature in the extracts? How are the themes presented to the audience? What issues might Shakespeare want his audience to think about?	
The language of the text What language devices are used? What is the effect of the language on the audience? How is punctuation used for dramatic effect? What mood is created? How is the language used by the characters reflective of their personalities?	
Text in performance *Atmosphere* - How would you create it? stage / lighting / colour / spotlights / fog / music / effects / levels *Characterisation* - Position / Movement / Costume / Tone of voice / Body language / Emphasis of key words *Advice to the actors* - How should they communicate to themselves / the other characters / the audience?	

MUCH ADO 2007
© BADGER PUBLISHING

Act 1, Scene 1 (40-78)

MESSENGER	He hath done good service, lady, in these wars.	40
BEATRICE	You had musty victual, and he hath holp to eat it. He is a very valiant trencher-man; he hath an excellent stomach.	
MESSENGER	And a good soldier too, lady.	
BEATRICE	And a good soldier to a lady. But what is he to a lord?	45
MESSENGER	A lord to a lord, a man to a man, stuffed with all honourable virtues.	
BEATRICE	It is so, indeed; he is no less than a stuffed man. But for the stuffing – well, we are all mortal.	
LEONATO	You must not, sir, mistake my niece. There is a kind of merry war betwixt Signior Benedick and her. They never meet but there's a skirmish of wit between them.	50
BEATRICE	Alas, he gets nothing by that. In our last conflict four of his five wits went halting off, and now is the whole man governed with one: so that if he have wit enough to keep himself warm, let him bear it for a difference between himself and his horse; for it is all the wealth that he hath left, to be known a reasonable creature. Who is his companion now? He hath every month a new sworn brother.	55 60
MESSENGER	Is't possible?	
BEATRICE	Very easily possible. He wears his faith but as the fashion of his hat: it ever changes with the next block.	
MESSENGER	I see, lady, the gentleman is not in your books.	
BEATRICE	No: an he were, I would burn my study. But, I pray you, who is his companion? Is there no young squarer now that will make a voyage with him to the devil?	65
MESSENGER	He is most in the company of the right noble Claudio.	
BEATRICE	O Lord, he will hang upon him like a disease. He is sooner caught than the pestilence, and the taker runs presently mad. God help the noble Claudio! If he have caught the Benedick, it will cost him a thousand pound ere 'a be cured.	70
MESSENGER	I will hold friends with you, lady.	
BEATRICE	Do, good friend.	75
LEONATO	*You* will never run mad, niece.	
BEATRICE	No, not till a hot January.	
MESSENGER	Don Pedro is approached.	

Reproduced with permission from the Longman School Shakespeare
edition © Pearson Education Ltd (2004)

MUCH ADO 2007

Responding to the assessment focuses
Act 1, Scene 1 (40-78)

Assessment focus and prompts	Student response
Motivation and behaviour What are the characters feeling? Why? Who influences them? Are their actions typical of them? How do the other characters react to them? What impact do their actions in this scene have on the rest of the play? How would the audience react to them?	
Ideas, themes and issues Which themes feature in the extracts? How are the themes presented to the audience? What issues might Shakespeare want his audience to think about?	
The language of the text What language devices are used? What is the effect of the language on the audience? How is punctuation used for dramatic effect? What mood is created? How is the language used by the characters reflective of their personalities?	
Text in performance *Atmosphere* - How would you create it? stage / lighting / colour / spotlights / fog / music / effects / levels *Characterisation* - Position / Movement / Costume / Tone of voice / Body language / Emphasis of key words *Advice to the actors* - How should they communicate to themselves / the other characters / the audience?	

MUCH ADO 2007
© BADGER PUBLISHING

Act 1, Scene 1 (79-123)

Enter DON PEDRO, CLAUDIO, BENEDICK, BALTHASAR, and DON JOHN the bastard (Don Pedro's half-brother).

DON PEDRO	Good Signior Leonato, are you come to meet your trouble? The fashion of the world is to avoid cost, and you encounter it.	80
LEONATO	Never came trouble to my house in the likeness of your Grace. For trouble being gone, comfort should remain; but when you depart from me sorrow abides, and happiness takes his leave.	85
DON PEDRO	You embrace your charge too willingly. (*Indicating HERO*) I think this is your daughter.	
LEONATO	Her mother hath many times told me so.	
BENEDICK	Were you in doubt, sir, that you asked her?	
LEONATO	Signior Benedick, no; for then were you a child.	90
DON PEDRO	You have it full, Benedick: we may guess by this what you are, being a man. Truly, the lady fathers herself. (*To HERO*) Be happy, lady; for you are like an honourable father.	
BENEDICK	If Signior Leonato be her father, she would not have his head on her shoulders for all Messina, as like him as she is.	95

DON PEDRO and LEONATO move aside to talk.

BEATRICE	I wonder that you will still be talking, Signior Benedick. Nobody marks you.	
BENEDICK	What, my dear Lady Disdain! Are you yet living?	100
BEATRICE	Is it possible disdain should die while she hath such meet food to feed it as Signior Benedick? Courtesy itself must convert to disdain, if you come in her presence.	
BENEDICK	Then is courtesy a turncoat. But it is certain I am loved of all ladies, only you excepted; and I would I could find in my heart that I had not a hard heart, for, truly, I love none.	105
BEATRICE	A dear happiness to women: they would else have been troubled with a pernicious suitor! I thank God and my cold blood, I am of your humour for that. I had rather hear my dog bark at a crow than a man swear he loves me.	110
BENEDICK	God keep your ladyship still in that mind! So some gentleman or other shall 'scape a predestinate scratched face.	115
BEATRICE	Scratching could not make it worse, and 'twere such a face as yours were.	
BENEDICK	Well, you are a rare parrot-teacher.	
BEATRICE	A bird of my tongue is better than a beast of yours.	
BENEDICK	I would my horse had the speed of your tongue, and so good a continuer. But keep your way, a' God's name. I have done.	120
BEATRICE	You always end with a jade's trick: I know you of old.	

MUCH ADO 2007

Responding to the assessment focuses
Act 1, Scene 1 (79-123)

Assessment focus and prompts	Student response
Motivation and behaviour What are the characters feeling? Why? Who influences them? Are their actions typical of them? How do the other characters react to them? What impact do their actions in this scene have on the rest of the play? How would the audience react to them?	
Ideas, themes and issues Which themes feature in the extracts? How are the themes presented to the audience? What issues might Shakespeare want his audience to think about?	
The language of the text What language devices are used? What is the effect of the language on the audience? How is punctuation used for dramatic effect? What mood is created? How is the language used by the characters reflective of their personalities?	
Text in performance *Atmosphere* - How would you create it? stage / lighting / colour / spotlights / fog / music / effects / levels *Characterisation* - Position / Movement / Costume / Tone of voice / Body language / Emphasis of key words *Advice to the actors* - How should they communicate to themselves / the other characters / the audience?	

Act 2, Scene 1 (183-229)

Enter DON PEDRO, with LEONATO and HERO following.

DON PEDRO	(*To BENEDICK*) Now signior, where's the Count? Did you see him?	
BENEDICK	Troth, my lord, I have played the part of Lady Fame. I found him here as melancholy as a lodge in a warren. I told him, and I think I told him true, that your Grace had got the good will of this young lady; and I offered him my company to a willow-tree, either to make him a garland, as being forsaken, or to bind him up a rod, as being worthy to be whipped.	185 190
DON PEDRO	To be whipped! What's his fault?	
BENEDICK	The flat transgression of a schoolboy – who being overjoyed with finding a bird's nest, shows it his companion, and he steals it.	 195
DON PEDRO	Wilt thou make a trust a transgression? The transgression is in the stealer.	
BENEDICK	Yet it had not been amiss the rod had been made, and the garland too: for the garland he might have worn himself, and the rod he might have bestowed on you, who, as I take it, have stolen his bird's nest.	 200
DON PEDRO	I will but teach them to sing, and restore them to the owner.	
BENEDICK	If their singing answer your saying, by my faith you say honestly.	 205
DON PEDRO	The Lady Beatrice hath a quarrel to you: the gentleman that danced with her told her she is much wronged by you.	
BENEDICK	O, she misused me past the endurance of a block! An oak but with one green leaf on it would have answered her. My very visor began to assume life and scold with her. She told me, not thinking I had been myself, that I was the Prince's jester, that I was duller than a great thaw – huddling jest upon jest with such impossible conveyance upon me that I stood like a man at a mark, with a whole army shooting at me. She speaks poniards, and every word stabs. If her breath were as terrible as her terminations, there were no living near her: she would infect to the north star. I would not marry her, though she were endowed with all that Adam had left him before he transgressed. She would have made Hercules have turned spit, yea, and have cleft his club to make the fire too. Come, talk not of her. You shall find her the infernal Até in good apparel. I would to God some scholar would conjure her. For certainly, while she is here, a man may live as quiet in hell as in a sanctuary, and people sin upon purpose because they would go thither. So indeed, all disquiet, horror, and perturbation follows her.	210 215 220 225

Responding to the assessment focuses
Act 2, Scene 1 (183-229)

Assessment focus and prompts	Student response
Motivation and behaviour What are the characters feeling? Why? Who influences them? Are their actions typical of them? How do the other characters react to them? What impact do their actions in this scene have on the rest of the play? How would the audience react to them?	
Ideas, themes and issues Which themes feature in the extracts? How are the themes presented to the audience? What issues might Shakespeare want his audience to think about?	
The language of the text What language devices are used? What is the effect of the language on the audience? How is punctuation used for dramatic effect? What mood is created? How is the language used by the characters reflective of their personalities?	
Text in performance *Atmosphere* - How would you create it? stage / lighting / colour / spotlights / fog / music / effects / levels *Characterisation* - Position / Movement / Costume / Tone of voice / Body language / Emphasis of key words *Advice to the actors* - How should they communicate to themselves / the other characters / the audience?	

MUCH ADO 2007
© BADGER PUBLISHING

Act 2, Scene 1 (230-274)

Enter CLAUDIO and BEATRICE.

DON PEDRO	Look, here she comes.	230
BENEDICK	Will your Grace command me any service to the world's end? I will go on the slightest errand now to the Antipodes that you can devise to send me on. I will fetch you a tooth-picker now from the furthest inch of Asia; bring you the length of Prester John's foot; fetch you a hair off the great Cham's beard; do you any embassage to the Pigmies – rather than hold three words' conference with this harpy. You have no employment for me?	235
DON PEDRO	None, but to desire your good company.	240
BENEDICK	O God, sir, here's a dish I love not. I cannot endure my Lady Tongue.	

Exit BENEDICK.

DON PEDRO	Come, lady, come. You have lost the heart of Signior Benedick.	
BEATRICE	Indeed, my lord, he lent it me awhile, and I gave him use for it, a double heart for his single one. Marry, once before he won it of me with false dice: therefore your Grace may well say I have lost it.	245
DON PEDRO	You have put him down, lady, you have put him down.	
BEATRICE	So I would not he should do me, my lord, lest I should prove the mother of fools. I have brought Count Claudio, whom you sent me to seek.	250
DON PEDRO	Why, how now, Count! Wherefore are you sad?	
CLAUDIO	Not sad, my lord.	
DON PEDRO	How then? Sick?	255
CLAUDIO	Neither, my lord.	
BEATRICE	The Count is neither sad, nor sick, nor merry, nor well; but civil count, civil as an orange, and something of that jealous complexion.	
DON PEDRO	I'faith, lady, I think your blazon to be true; though, I'll be sworn, if he be so, his conceit is false. Here, Claudio, I have wooed in thy name, and fair Hero is won. I have broke with her father, and his good will obtained. Name the day of marriage, and God give thee joy!	260
LEONATO	Count, take of me my daughter, and with her my fortunes. His Grace hath made the match and all grace say Amen to it!	265
BEATRICE	Speak, Count, 'tis your cue.	
CLAUDIO	Silence is the perfectest herald of joy. I were but little happy, if I could say how much. Lady, as you are mine, I am yours: I give away myself for you and dote upon the exchange.	270
BEATRICE	Speak, cousin – or, if you cannot, stop his mouth with a kiss, and let not him speak neither.	

MUCH ADO 2007

© BADGER PUBLISHING

Responding to the assessment focuses
Act 2, Scene 1 (230-274)

Assessment focus and prompts	Student response
Motivation and behaviour What are the characters feeling? Why? Who influences them? Are their actions typical of them? How do the other characters react to them? What impact do their actions in this scene have on the rest of the play? How would the audience react to them?	
Ideas, themes and issues Which themes feature in the extracts? How are the themes presented to the audience? What issues might Shakespeare want his audience to think about?	
The language of the text What language devices are used? What is the effect of the language on the audience? How is punctuation used for dramatic effect? What mood is created? How is the language used by the characters reflective of their personalities?	
Text in performance *Atmosphere* - How would you create it? stage / lighting / colour / spotlights / fog / music / effects / levels *Characterisation* - Position / Movement / Costume / Tone of voice / Body language / Emphasis of key words *Advice to the actors* - How should they communicate to themselves / the other characters / the audience?	

MUCH ADO 2007
© BADGER PUBLISHING

DON PEDRO	In faith, lady, you have a merry heart.	275
BEATRICE	Yea, my lord; I thank it, poor fool, it keeps on the windy side of care. My cousin tells him in his ear that he is in her heart.	
CLAUDIO	And so she doth, cousin.	
BEATRICE	Good Lord, for alliance! Thus goes everyone to the world but I, and I am sunburnt. I may sit in a corner and cry 'Heigh-ho for a husband!'	280
DON PEDRO	Lady Beatrice, I will get you one.	
BEATRICE	I would rather have one of your father's getting. Hath your Grace ne'er a brother like you? Your father got excellent husbands, if a maid could come by them.	285
DON PEDRO	Will you have *me*, lady?	
BEATRICE	No, my lord, unless I might have another for working-days. Your Grace is too costly to wear every day. But I beseech your Grace, pardon me: I was born to speak all mirth and no matter.	290
DON PEDRO	Your silence most offends me, and to be merry best becomes you; for, out of question, you were born in a merry hour.	
BEATRICE	No, sure, my lord, my mother cried. But then there was a star danced, and under that was I born. Cousins, God give you joy!	295
LEONATO	Niece, will you look to those things I told you of?	
BEATRICE	I cry you mercy, uncle. (*To DON PEDRO*) By your Grace's pardon.	300

Exit BEATRICE.

DON PEDRO	By my troth, a pleasant-spirited lady.	
LEONATO	There's little of the melancholy element in her, my lord. She is never sad but when she sleeps, and not ever sad then: for I have heard my daughter say, she hath often dreamt of unhappiness and waked herself with laughing.	305
DON PEDRO	She cannot endure to hear tell of a husband.	
LEONATO	O, by no means. She mocks all her wooers out of suit.	
DON PEDRO	She were an excellent wife for Benedick.	
LEONATO	O Lord, my lord, if they were but a week married, they would talk themselves mad.	310

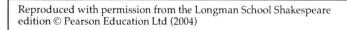

MUCH ADO 2007
© BADGER PUBLISHING

Responding to the assessment focuses
Act 2, Scene 1 (275-310)

Assessment focus and prompts	Student response
Motivation and behaviour What are the characters feeling? Why? Who influences them? Are their actions typical of them? How do the other characters react to them? What impact do their actions in this scene have on the rest of the play? How would the audience react to them?	
Ideas, themes and issues Which themes feature in the extracts? How are the themes presented to the audience? What issues might Shakespeare want his audience to think about?	
The language of the text What language devices are used? What is the effect of the language on the audience? How is punctuation used for dramatic effect? What mood is created? How is the language used by the characters reflective of their personalities?	
Text in performance *Atmosphere* - How would you create it? stage / lighting / colour / spotlights / fog / music / effects / levels *Characterisation* - Position / Movement / Costume / Tone of voice / Body language / Emphasis of key words *Advice to the actors* - How should they communicate to themselves / the other characters / the audience?	

MUCH ADO 2007
© BADGER PUBLISHING

Act 2, Scene 1 (311-end)

DON PEDRO	Count Claudio, when mean you to go to church?
CLAUDIO	Tomorrow, my lord. Time goes on crutches, till love have all his rites.
LEONATO	Not till Monday, my dear son, which is hence a just seven-night – and a time too brief, too, to have all things answer my mind.
DON PEDRO	Come, you shake the head at so long a breathing – but I warrant thee, Claudio, the time shall not go dully by us. I will in the interim undertake one of Hercules' labours – which is, to bring Signior Benedick and the Lady Beatrice into a mountain of affection, the one with the other. I would fain have it a match; and I doubt not but to fashion it, if you three will but minister such assistance as I shall give you direction.
LEONATO	My lord, I am for you, though it cost me ten nights' watchings.
CLAUDIO	And I, my lord.
DON PEDRO	And you too, gentle Hero?
HERO	I will do any modest office, my lord, to help my cousin to a good husband.
DON PEDRO	And Benedick is not the unhopefullest husband that I know. Thus far can I praise him: he is of a noble strain, of approved valour and confirmed honesty. I will teach you how to humour your cousin, that she shall fall in love with Benedick. And I, with your two helps, will so practise on Benedick that, in despite of his quick wit and his queasy stomach, he shall fall in love with Beatrice. If we can do this, Cupid is no longer an archer: his glory shall be ours, for we are the only love-gods. Go in with me, and I will tell you my drift.

315

320

325

330

335

340

Exeunt.

MUCH ADO 2007

Responding to the assessment focuses
Act 2, Scene 1 (311-end)

Assessment focus and prompts	Student response
Motivation and behaviour What are the characters feeling? Why? Who influences them? Are their actions typical of them? How do the other characters react to them? What impact do their actions in this scene have on the rest of the play? How would the audience react to them?	
Ideas, themes and issues Which themes feature in the extracts? How are the themes presented to the audience? What issues might Shakespeare want his audience to think about?	
The language of the text What language devices are used? What is the effect of the language on the audience? How is punctuation used for dramatic effect? What mood is created? How is the language used by the characters reflective of their personalities?	
Text in performance *Atmosphere* - How would you create it? stage / lighting / colour / spotlights / fog / music / effects / levels *Characterisation* - Position / Movement / Costume / Tone of voice / Body language / Emphasis of key words *Advice to the actors* - How should they communicate to themselves / the other characters / the audience?	

MUCH ADO 2007
© BADGER PUBLISHING

Chapter 7
Exam preparation

- One essay question (no choice).
- 45 minutes to complete essay.
- Question will be based on an extract from the key scenes.

Act 1, Scene 1 (1-139) - Act 2, Scene 1 (183-340)

Being familiar with the information on exam day
Before you begin the exam, you need to familiarise yourself with the information that is on the desk in front of you:

- Question booklet
- Answer booklet

Your question booklet is divided into the following sections:

Front page – exam information	Page 2 - exam question with details of the key scenes you need to focus on; i.e.	Page 3 – end
Shakespeare paper Please read this page, but do not open the booklet until your teacher tells you to start. The test is 45 minutes long. It has one task which assesses your reading and understanding of *Much Ado about Nothing*, and has 18 marks.	**Much Ado about Nothing** Act 1, Scene 1 (1-139) and Act 2, Scene 1 (183-340) **How does Shakespeare use language to reveal the different attitudes held towards love and marriage?** *Support your ideas by referring to both extracts.*	Copies of the key scenes themselves. During planning, brief notes should be made on these that relate to the question set.

Using time effectively during an exam

As you have only 45 minutes for this question, you need to plan your time carefully. The following is advised:

0-5	5 minutes annotate the exam question, locate relevant quotes from the scenes and devise a brief essay plan.
5-40	35 minutes – write the essay, remembering to always refer to the question in every paragraph, as well as each of the printed key scenes.
40-45	5 minutes to check over your essay to correct simple mistakes and add extra information you may have left out. Remember it is a test of your reading, therefore it is better to use this time to add information rather than correct simple mistakes.

Annotating the exam question

It is crucial that, before you begin the exam, you make sense of the question in order to direct your plan and essay. Many students will write a brilliant essay on a question that wasn't actually set or on scenes that they weren't asked to write about. The examiner will only award marks if you have answered the question set and focused on the scenes mentioned.

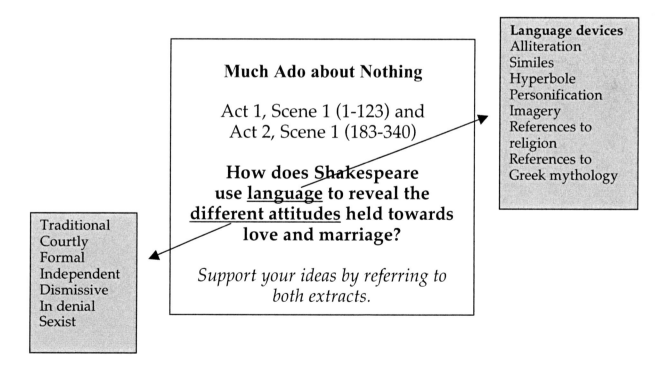

Language devices
Alliteration
Similes
Hyperbole
Personification
Imagery
References to religion
References to Greek mythology

Much Ado about Nothing

Act 1, Scene 1 (1-123) and
Act 2, Scene 1 (183-340)

How does Shakespeare use language to reveal the different attitudes held towards love and marriage?

Support your ideas by referring to both extracts.

Traditional
Courtly
Formal
Independent
Dismissive
In denial
Sexist

MUCH ADO 2007
© BADGER PUBLISHING

Practical exam tips

It is very easy to lose track and focus during an exam.

Some suggestions to overcome this are shown below:

- Every 5/10 minutes during your essay, look back at the essay question and refer to your plan.
- Use the key words from the question in every paragraph to ensure you are answering the question set.
- Use a topic sentence at the beginning of every paragraph which focuses on the question set.
- Make sure you are using quotes from the key scenes to support your points.
- In the margin, copy the key word(s) from the question every 10 lines as a reminder to stay focused.
- Refer to both extracts during your analysis, commenting on how a character/theme may have changed and developed from one scene to the other. You need to explore the reasons for this change and how this is communicated in the different extracts.
- Do not retell the plot – the examiner will know it well and can only award marks for your understanding of the key scenes.
- Remember that the examiner will be assessing your ability to:
  - focus on the question
  - use well chosen references to justify points made
  - show clear understanding of Shakespeare's use of language and the impact on the audience

Essay planning

There is not one correct way of writing an essay plan – the important thing is that you write one that:

- relates to the key words in the exam question
- helps to organise your thoughts during the essay

Over the page is an example of a brief essay plan – notice that it has been structured in a way that relates directly to the question set and the key scenes.

Example of an essay plan

Act 1, Scene 1 (1-123) and Act 2, Scene 1 (183-end)

How are the conflicts between men and women explored in these scenes?

Conflicts between men and women	
Act 1, Scene 1 (1-139)	**Act 2, Scene 1 (183-end)**
• Jovial exchange between Beatrice and Leonato • No voice of Hero – controlled by father, Leonato • Significant contrast between Hero's relationship with father and Beatrice's • Arrogance of men (challenging Cupid) • Traditional roles challenged • Good soldier to a lady • Merry war (Don Pedro) • Increasing level of insults hide depth of feelings • Question of sincerity • Seemingly joint ambitions to stay unmarried – hints at being defensive • Hints at previous relationship (Jade's trick)	• Love so fragile (Claudio) • Frustration/jealousy of others' happiness • Effects of (seemingly) unrequited love • Hero seen as commodity that is to be won and owned • Previous masked ball developed the conflict • Theme of deception running through the male/female conflict • Conflict between Benedick and Beatrice developed and now more personal and vicious • Anger used as defence mechanism to avoid upset (Beatrice) • Revelations of previous rejection – helps to explain Beatrice's actions towards Benedick • Sharp contrast between male/female relationships of Benedick/Beatrice and Claudio/Hero • Obsession with marriage – feeling that those unmarried need to be fixed up • Conflict attempted to be resolved through deception

You could use these bullet points to begin your paragraphs – they can act as topic sentences. These brief notes have been made after quickly scanning through the set scenes; as you do this, it is vital that you annotate the section that you want to refer to and use quotes from.

Annotating the extracts

It is not enough to simply underline as you may forget why you have done so – make a brief note next to the annotation to help when writing the essay.

For example:

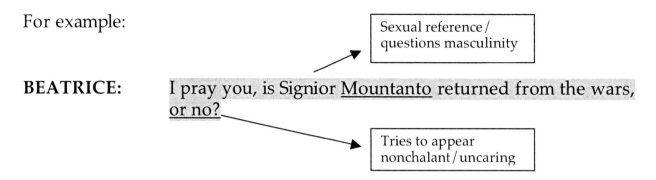

BEATRICE: I pray you, is Signior Mountanto returned from the wars, or no?

Sexual reference / questions masculinity

Tries to appear nonchalant / uncaring

Writing the exam question

How to improve sentence structure and written expression

Although this exam is a test of your reading skills, you will need to ensure that you express yourself in a clear and concise way in order to communicate your thoughts and feelings to the examiner. Remember that your examiner will have hundreds of scripts to mark and will not have the patience and understanding that your teacher will have. Varying your sentence structures and sentence starters will also help to make your writing more interesting and engaging for the examiner, though remember it's an analytical piece that's required – not descriptive.

It's not enough to make the writing make sense to you as you cannot presume the examiner will always follow your line of thought unless you make it clear; moreover, well structured sentences and clearly separated paragraphs that use topic sentences are a signal to the examiner that the script belongs to a level 5 student at least.

Experiment with varying your sentence starters; use adjectives, verbs and connectives as it will help to extend your sentence and display greater knowledge and analysis. On the next page are a list of sentence starters, connecting words and phrases that will help you to express your ideas clearly. Try to avoid beginning every sentence with the name of the character you are writing about or the scene reference. These are generic phrases which will need to be applied to the question set.

How to improve sentence structure and written expression

Sentence starters	<ul><li>Whilst seeming highly confident and single minded externally, Beatrice's insecurity…</li><li>Shakespeare presents the diverse relationships between men and women through his exploration of…</li><li>The audience would feel anticipation at the prospect of…</li><li>Deception is explored through the previous misuse of the masked ball, which…</li></ul>
Connecting words to use when adding a point	<ul><li>Also</li><li>In addition</li><li>Furthermore</li><li>Moreover</li></ul> <ul><li>Another key point is</li><li>As well as</li><li>What is more</li></ul>
Connecting words to use when making a comparison	<ul><li>However</li><li>Whereas</li><li>On the other hand</li><li>In contrast</li><li>Nevertheless</li></ul> <ul><li>On the contrary</li><li>Otherwise</li><li>Despite this</li><li>Alternatively</li><li>Unlike</li></ul>
Explaining the intended effect on the audience	This… <ul><li>shows</li><li>reveals</li><li>reflects</li><li>implies</li><li>reinforces</li><li>represents</li><li>echoes</li><li>communicates</li></ul> <ul><li>indicates</li><li>demonstrates</li><li>symbolises</li><li>epitomises</li><li>shows the audience</li><li>reveals Shakespeare's thoughts on</li></ul>

MUCH ADO 2007
© BADGER PUBLISHING

Structuring your ideas clearly

The table below demonstrates how you can organise your thoughts in a well structured way – making it easier for the examiner to understand your points and see that you are using evidence correctly. Furthermore, it is crucial that, when you use a quotation, you explain what it reveals about the character or theme that you are commenting on. You will notice that the structure used below is based on the way that the examiner will mark your work.

Act 1, Scene 1 (1-123) and Act 2, Scene 1 (183-end)
How are the conflicts between men and women explored in these scenes?

Sentence structure	Paragraph 1
Focus on the question using varied sentence starter/connective	*The dutiful behaviour of Hero towards her father, Leonato, and prospective husband, Claudio, is in sharp contrast to the vibrant and free reign that Beatrice has towards all the men who know her, in particular Leonato, who remarks:*
Well chosen references used to justify points made	*"Faith, niece, you tax Signior Benedick too much; but he'll be meet with you, I doubt it not"*
Clear understanding of Shakespeare's use of language and the impact on the audience	*Leonato's response to Beatrice's early insults towards Benedick are a clear indication of the equal status she holds with men in the play.*
Sentence structure	Paragraph 2
Focus on the question using varied sentence starter/connective	*This is in sharp contrast to Hero's relationship with her father and Claudio which is based on duty, formality and status. This is revealed when Leonato says to Claudio:*
Well chosen references used to justify points made	*"Count, take of me my daughter, and with her my fortunes"*
Clear understanding of Shakespeare's use of language and the impact on the audience	*Shakespeare wants his audience to consider the role of women during this time; Hero is presented as a commodity for male usage – Leonato is pleased with her marrying a noble Count and Claudio will be receiving all her father's wealth.*

MUCH ADO 2007
© BADGER PUBLISHING

Essay writing frame

Below is a blank writing frame that you could use for the sample exam questions as well as a revision tool for your Shakespeare paper. It is important that you do not become over reliant on any form of writing frame – just make sure you express your ideas clearly, use evidence and focus on the question set.

Sentence structure	Paragraph ( )
▪ Focus on the question using varied sentence starter/connective	
▪ Well chosen references used to justify points made	
▪ Clear understanding of Shakespeare's use of language and the impact on the audience	
Sentence structure	**Paragraph ( )**
▪ Focus on the question using varied sentence starter/connective	
▪ Well chosen references used to justify points made	
▪ Clear understanding of Shakespeare's use of language and the impact on the audience	

MUCH ADO 2007
© BADGER PUBLISHING

Chapter 8
Sample exam questions

In this chapter, there are five sample exams based on the key scenes and written in the same format as the real exam. In order to replicate the exam conditions, you will also need to supply the key scenes with the exams so that students can easily refer to them when answering the question.

The questions are below and you will notice that they are spread between the 4 assessment focuses.

Sample paper	Question	Assessment focus
A	Act 1, Scene 1 (1-123) & Act 2, Scene 1 (183-end) How does Shakespeare use language to reveal the tensions that exist within these scenes?	The language of the text
B	Act 1, Scene 1 (1-123) & Act 2, Scene 1 (183-end) How are Beatrice's attitudes to men explored in these scenes?	Ideas, themes and issues
C	Act 1, Scene 1 (1-123) & Act 2, Scene 1 (183-end) What does Shakespeare want to communicate about the roles of men and women in these scenes?	Motivation and behaviour
D	Act 1, Scene 1 (1-123) & Act 2, Scene 1 (183-end) You have been asked to direct these scenes. What advice would you give to the actor playing Benedick on how to best communicate his thoughts and feelings to the audience?	The text in performance
E	Act 1, Scene 1 (1-123) & Act 2, Scene 1 (183-end) How does the theme of deception play such an important part in these scenes?	Ideas, themes and issues

For each question, students are asked to support their ideas by referring to both extracts – remind them about this before they begin. There is a mark scheme and exemplar responses in Chapter 9.

Much Ado about Nothing

En

Key Stage 3

Levels

4-7

Sample Paper A

Shakespeare paper

Please read this page, but do not open the booklet until your teacher tells you to start.

- The test is 45 minutes long.

- It has one task which assesses your reading and understanding of *Much Ado about Nothing*, and has 18 marks.

MUCH ADO 2007
© BADGER PUBLISHING

Sample Paper A

Reading Task

You have 45 minutes for this section.

Much Ado about Nothing

Act 1, Scene 1 (1-123) & Act 2, Scene 1 (183-end)

How does Shakespeare use language to reveal the tensions that exist within these scenes?

Support your ideas by referring to both extracts.

(18 marks)   *Q1*

MUCH ADO 2007
© BADGER PUBLISHING

Much Ado about Nothing

En

Key Stage 3

Levels

4-7

Sample Paper B

Shakespeare paper

Please read this page, but do not open the booklet until your teacher tells you to start.

- The test is 45 minutes long.

- It has one task which assesses your reading and understanding of *Much Ado about Nothing*, and has 18 marks.

MUCH ADO 2007
© BADGER PUBLISHING

Reading Task

You have 45 minutes for this section.

Much Ado about Nothing

Act 1, Scene 1 (1-123) & Act 2, Scene 1 (183-end)

How are Beatrice's attitudes to men explored in these scenes?

Support your ideas by referring to both extracts.

(18 marks)   *Q1*

Much Ado about Nothing

En

Key Stage 3

Levels

4-7

Sample Paper C

Shakespeare paper

Please read this page, but do not open the booklet until your teacher tells you to start.

- The test is 45 minutes long.

- It has one task which assesses your reading and understanding of *Much Ado about Nothing*, and has 18 marks.

MUCH ADO 2007
© BADGER PUBLISHING

Sample Paper C

Reading Task

You have 45 minutes for this section.

Much Ado about Nothing

Act 1, Scene 1 (1-123) & Act 2, Scene 1 (183-end)

What does Shakespeare want to communicate about the roles of men and women in these scenes?

Support your ideas by referring to both extracts.

(18 marks)   *Q1*

MUCH ADO 2007
© BADGER PUBLISHING

Much Ado about Nothing

En

Key Stage 3

Levels

4-7

Sample Paper D

Shakespeare paper

Please read this page, but do not open the booklet until your teacher tells you to start.

- The test is 45 minutes long.

- It has one task which assesses your reading and understanding of *Much Ado about Nothing*, and has 18 marks.

Sample Paper D

Reading Task

You have 45 minutes for this section.

Much Ado about Nothing

Act 1, Scene 1 (1-123) & Act 2, Scene 1 (183-end)

You have been asked to direct these scenes.

What advice would you give to the actor playing Benedick on how to best communicate his thoughts and feelings to the audience?

Support your ideas by referring to both extracts.

(18 marks)   *Q1*

Much Ado about Nothing

En

Key Stage 3

Levels

4-7

MUCH ADO 2007
© BADGER PUBLISHING

Sample Paper E

Shakespeare paper

Please read this page, but do not open the booklet until your teacher tells you to start.

- The test is 45 minutes long.

- It has one task which assesses your reading and understanding of *Much Ado about Nothing*, and has 18 marks.

Sample Paper E

Reading Task

You have 45 minutes for this section.

Much Ado about Nothing

Act 1, Scene 1 (1-123) & Act 2, Scene 1 (183-end)

How does the theme of deception play such an important part in these scenes?

Support your ideas by referring to both extracts.

(18 marks)   Q1

MUCH ADO 2007
© BADGER PUBLISHING

Chapter 9

Mark scheme, including explanation and exemplar responses

Reading Paper mark scheme

Band	Reading criteria	Marks available	Approx level
1	Simple facts retold. Misunderstanding may be evident. Answers partly relevant. Parts of text may be copied.	1 2 3	N
2	Little explanation, showing some awareness. Comments made, but mainly plot level. Broad references used that may lack relevance.	4 5 6	3
3	General understanding shown, yet points undeveloped. Limited awareness of language, with paraphrasing used. There are some relevant references to the text to illustrate points made.	7 8 9	4
4	Some discussion evident, though inconsistent in quality. Awareness of the effects of language. Ideas developed by relevant references to the text.	10 11 12	5
5	Clear focus on task. Clear understanding of the use of language. Well-chosen references used to support points.	13 14 15	6
6	Coherent analysis and insight shown consistently. Appreciation of the effects of language. Precisely selected references are integrated into the well-developed argument.	16 17 18	7

In order to make sense of this mark scheme, it is useful to divide up the sections to see progression more clearly. The examiner will be testing the following skills:
- Focus on the question
- Use of well chosen references
- Understanding of language

On page 85, the mark scheme is divided into sections based on these skills, which should help clarify these points.

The mark scheme explained

The Shakespeare mark scheme is personalised each year for the particular question that has been asked; however, there are common elements to each mark boundary which we will now explore. It is important to share this information with students in order for them to grasp what is expected of them in the exam and how they can move to the next level. Furthermore, it will help your department to support Assessment for Learning.

Broadly speaking, the mark scheme is divided into 6 bands; although these do not strictly translate into specific reading levels, it can be assumed that the six bands relate from N (below Level 3) to Level 7.

The reading level that the student is awarded will depend largely on how they perform in their reading paper, as this is worth 32 marks, whereas the Shakespeare question is only worth 18 marks.

Band	Approximate reading level
1	N
2	3
3	4
4	5
5	6
6	7

Over the page is a mark scheme for the Shakespeare paper which can be applied to any sample exam you wish to use. Notice the change in vocabulary that occurs between the levels – it is crucial that students know how to move to the next level and how this translates into their own targets.

MUCH ADO 2007
© BADGER PUBLISHING

Breaking down the mark scheme

Band	Focus	Understanding	References	Approx level
1	Simple facts retold. Misunderstanding may be evident.	None shown.	Parts of text may be copied.	N
2	Little explanation, showing some awareness.	Comments made, but mainly plot level.	Broad references used that may lack relevance.	3
3	Some discussion evident, though inconsistent in quality.	Awareness of the effects of language.	Ideas developed by relevant references to the text.	4
4	General understanding shown, yet points undeveloped.	Limited awareness of language, with paraphrasing used.	There are some relevant references to the text to illustrate points made.	5
5	Clear focus on task.	Clear understanding of the use of language.	Well-chosen references used to support points.	6
6	Coherent analysis and insight shown consistently.	Appreciation of the effects of language.	Precisely selected references are integrated into the well-developed argument.	7

MUCH ADO 2007
© BADGER PUBLISHING

Examples of students' work at each level (1)

Below is a chart which highlights the key features of the mark boundaries, with example responses at each level. This can be used to support Assessment for Learning in the classroom, especially through peer and self-assessment and the sharing of learning objectives with the students. One idea is to cut these up and ask students to place them in the correct order, justifying their views by annotating aspects from the mark scheme that match the marking criteria.

The levelled responses are based on the question:

Act 1, Scene 1 (1-123) and Act 2, Scene 1 (183-end)
How are Beatrice's attitudes to men explored in these scenes?

B= Band   M= Mark awarded   L= approximate Level

B	Examples of students' work at each level	M	L
1	*Beatrice likes leonatoe and gets on with him yet doesnt like benidic because they fight*	*1* *2* *3*	*N*
2	*Beatrice likes the men in the scene except Benedick who she can't get on with. She says that he used to have her heart and later on he says that she used him.*	*4* *5* *6*	*3*
3	*Beatrice feels different towards Benedick than she does towards the other men. She laughs with Don Pedro yet she becomes angry when Benedick arrives, saying that he needs a scratched face.*	*7* *8* *9*	*4*
4	*Beatrice has a negative attitude towards a man loving her which is shown when she says "I had rather hear my dog bark at a crow than a man swear he loves me." She is confident when talking to Claudio in Act 2, Scene 1 "Speak, Count, 'tis your cue." This shows that she is not scared of men and can stand up for herself.*	*10* *11* *12*	*5*

MUCH ADO 2007
© BADGER PUBLISHING

Examples of students' work at each level (2)

B	Examples of students' work at each level	M	L
5	Beatrice's defensive attitude towards men is evident from the opening exchange she has with the messenger when she describes Benedick as "Signior Mountanto". This demonstrates that she is already preparing her attack on him before his arrival. Later on, in Act 2, Scene 1, we discover the reasons for this defensive stance when she hints at a previous relationship with Benedick "a double heart for his single one". The heart metaphor implies that Beatrice was mistreated and possibly rejected by Benedick in the past; therefore, her anger being vented is perhaps a sign that she is protecting herself from further rejection.	13 14 15	6
6	Beatrice's attitude towards men in these extracts varies considerably which demonstrates the full extent of Beatrice's complex personality. Early on she is humorous with a cutting edge "Is it possible disdain should die while she hath such meet food to feed it as Signior Benedick." She is determined to be recognised as an equal and can hold her own very easily on an intellectual and emotional level. In view of the historical and social context of this play, with an extremely male dominated society, her open antagonism and determination to not be controlled by a man would certainly have provoked a stronger reaction in the 16th century than today. However, Beatrice also reveals an insecure side on occasion, especially when she admits to being hurt by Benedick in the past "therefore your Grace may well say I have lost it". The audience would admire her free spirit, sympathise with her previous treatment and also recognise that her ability to hold court in a male dominated world is quite a remarkable achievement, saying much for her character and motivation. She is able to be released from the dutiful acts that her cousin has to engage in, flirt with Don Pedro, abuse Benedick, whilst taking centre stage when she feels necessary "Speak, Count, tis your cue."	16 17 18	7

MUCH ADO 2007
© BADGER PUBLISHING

I would like to dedicate this book to my wonderful
daughter Annabelle who makes everything else seem
much of ado!

Badger Publishing Limited
15 Wedgwood Gate,
Pin Green Industrial Estate,
Stevenage, Hertfordshire SG1 4SU
Telephone: 01438 356907
Fax: 01438 747015
www.badger-publishing.co.uk
enquiries@badger-publishing.co.uk

SAT Attack - Badger Test Guides
Key Stage 3 English – Assess Much Ado about Nothing with Focus 2007
ISBN 978 1 84691 092 0

Text © Jonathan Morgan 2006
Complete work © Badger Publishing Limited 2006

Publisher: David Jamieson
Editor: Paul Martin
Designer: Adam Wilmott
Illustrator: Roger Wade-Walker (Beehive Illustration)

Printed in the UK.

SAT ATTACK

KS3 Test Revision Guides from Badger Publishing

Supplies of Ammunition to help make your National Tests Mission Possible

KS3 English Test Revision Guides by Jonathan Morgan

Reading Student Book	ISBN 978 1 84424 422 5
Writing Student Book	ISBN 978 1 84424 423 2
Teacher Book for Reading and Writing	ISBN 978 1 84424 425 6
Teacher Book PDF CD	ISBN 978 1 84424 623 6
Macbeth Teacher Book – 2005 SATs	*ISBN 978 1 84424 424 9*
Assess Macbeth with Focus 2006	*ISBN 978 1 84424 676 2*

NEW for 2007!

Assess *The Tempest* with Focus 2007	ISBN 978 1 84691 091 3
Assess *Much Ado about Nothing* with Focus 2007	ISBN 978 1 84691 092 0
Assess *Richard III* with Focus 2007	ISBN 978 1 84691 093 7

KS3 Maths Test Revision Guides
by David Kent, Joan Knott, Colin Murray, Liz Rimmer

Student Book for Levels 3-6	ISBN 978 1 84424 408 9
Student Book for Levels 5-8	ISBN 978 1 84424 409 6
Teacher Book with Copymasters	ISBN 978 1 84424 410 2
Teacher Book PDF CD	ISBN 978 1 84424 622 9

Advice for students, tips on revision, help on achieving maximum marks, plenty of examples, explanation of marking and levels…

Fully supportive teacher notes, with sample tests, mark schemes, and Copymasters / OHTs.

Badger Publishing